CENTER OF THE STORM

THE BOMBING OF DUTCH HARBOR AND THE EXPERIENCE OF PATROL WING FOUR IN THE ALEUTIANS, SUMMER 1942.

BY JEFF DICKRELL

Pictorial Histories Publishing Co., Inc.
Missoula, MT

LIBRARY OF CONGRESS
CONTROL NUMBER 2001 135881

ISBN 1-57510-092-4
First Printing April 2002

Printed in Manitoba, Canada
by Hignell Book Printing

Typography and layout by Jan Taylor
Cover graphics by Egeler Design

Published for the
Museum of the Aleutians
Unalaska, Alaska
by
PICTORIAL HISTORIES PUBLISHING COMPANY, INC.
713 South Third West, Missoula, Montana 59801
(406) 549-8488   phpc@montana.com

INTRODUCTION

Jeff Dickrell

This book is a combination of many of my passions. Historic photographs, oral histories, World War II, airplanes and the Aleutian Islands all meet here. It has been my privilege to be involved with the men of Patrol Wing Four, and an honor to add to their story.

Unalaska/Dutch Harbor is a long way from the suburbs where I grew up, but it was there my father, a WW II vet, would haul the family off to air shows every summer. We would see the Blue Angels and the Pit Specials flying acrobatically overhead, but it was always the warbirds which drew my attention—the planes themselves, the P-51s, Spitfires and P-40s, but also the history behind them, their paint jobs and the men who flew them into harm's way. At a Confederate Air Force Show we watched, enthralled, as fighters buzzed the large, slow multi-engine behemoths. These were different animals, with fascinating stories behind them.

Local history is hard to come by in the Midwest. Anything that was something had been destroyed, paved over or made into a boutique. The landscape has been stripped of its past. It was from that place that I came to the Aleutians as the high school history teacher. Now here was a landscape which had history pouring out of its every crevice. Ruined buildings from the war remained. Barbed wire fences trip up hikers in the tall grass still. One lands on the runway carved out of Ballyhoo Mountain in 1942.

Most of downtown Unalaska was created after the war by dragging army "cabanas" down from the hills to replace homes destroyed when the local Aleut people were forcibly relocated for the duration of the war. An event which is still very much a part of their culture.

The history of their culture takes one back 10,000 years. Prior to the war, fox farming, sealing, whaling, sea otter hunting all had their booms and busts. Before the coming of the Russians in the 1750s the Unangan people lived in large villages, paddled skin boats of amazing complexity and created a wonderful culture, the remains of which are found right beneath our feet.

In the mid–1990s I located a map of the precise locations of where the Japanese bombs hit. That afternoon I rode my bike to a spot above the runway. Sure enough, there were five craters, some 35 feet across. There was no indication of their origin. The next day Rick Knecht, director of the Museum of the Aleutians, some of my students and I drove to the craters armed with shovels and a metal detector. Within minutes we dug out several sharp, jagged pieces of metal, shrapnel from the attacks on June 4, 1942. That is a history lesson none of us will forget.

About this time, The Monogram Company released a large–scale model of the PBY. I thought it would be a great project to build and paint a plane from the Aleutian Theater. I called a vet, Elmer Freeman, whom I had met at a WW II symposium in Anchorage. He had been selling his book *Those Navy Guys and their PBYs,* an account of his experiences as a crew member in Patrol Wing Four. We had talked then, and he remembered me. "Say El, what color were the interiors of your PBYs painted," I asked?

"Green" he replied.

"Yes, but what shade of green," I asked? I needed to know.

That began the stories. I had always been intrigued with the bombing of Dutch Harbor from a local point of view. Where did the bombs hit, what damage had been done, how many casualties, is there anything left from that event? I asked him pointed questions about Dutch Harbor. He hadn't really spent much time in town. He gave me another name. I called and was passed along until I contacted Ole Haugen, keeper of the unit's history. Ole was warm and receptive. He graciously sent me a list of names of men who were in the unit at the time of the bombing, with the best storytellers highlighted.

With no real purpose in mind, I mailed all the men on the list a letter asking for their story of the events surrounding the bombing of Dutch Harbor and the role of the Patrol Wing. The response was simply overwhelming. Daily I received letters detailing experiences 55 years past. I answered each one personally, with more questions and many thanks. I began an e—mail relationship with Bob Larson and Bill Theis. They were great about answering detailed questions about clothing, procedures and equipment.

Coinciding with my letter writing campaign, the City of Unalaska voted to build the Museum of the Aleutians. Another letter went out from me asking for donations in the form of photos, memorabilia and uniforms. Again the men of the Wing responded generously. By this time word had spread in our small town. People would make me open packages in the post office to see what new cool thing had been sent. I am glad to say that most of it makes up the WW II display today.

As the high school history teacher I take a small group of students to a Washington, DC tour program every spring. This allows me to spend time in the Still Pictures Division of the National Archives. A very modern and well indexed facility, it was a gold mine of images related to this story. The Navy was judicious in recording events as they happened. When a crewman told me about a particularly harrowing episode, I was able to find a photograph of his crew exiting the PBY, tense smiles as they pointed out bullet holes in the fuselage of their plane. Photos add immensely to the words of those who were there. Nearly 300 are included here, including many sent by veterans themselves.

In 1997 and 1999 I was able to attend reunions of the Patrol Wing. Putting faces to names was a treat, but to be accepted into their fold was an experience I will always treasure. I think they were thrilled that someone was interested, knew their story and was actually living in the Aleutians. For once we didn't have to waste adjectives trying to describe the weather of the Chain. We all knew too well. Sam Cobean, who won the Silver Star at Atka Island, stayed in the Navy after the war. Flying 30,000 feet over the chain in modern patrol plane on his way to Adak N.A.S. many years after the war, he did a lazy circle over Atka. "What the heck are you doing? There's nothing down there," his copilot said. Still gazing downwards he replied, "You wouldn't believe me if I told you".

Unalaska, Alaska, 2001

Note: Photos not credited are from the National Archives collection.

PROLOGUE

Burke Mees

I was not in the Aleutians during the war, in fact I was not born until 21 years after it ended. I do have some insights into the wartime PBY operations as I am currently living in Dutch Harbor, making my living flying the Aleutians in a twin–engine amphibian similar to a PBY. Peninsula Airways provides a scheduled passenger and mail service in the Eastern Aleutians with a Grumman Goose that was built in 1945 as a Navy JRF5.

Abundant relics from World War II still exist on these islands. They are part of the backdrop of our everyday lives here. At Dutch Harbor, concrete bunkers are still positioned along the beach to repel an invasion. There are still discernible craters from the 1942 bombing. At Chernofski, an occasional fishing boat still ties up to the old military dock that has fallen badly into disrepair. At Fort Glenn we still use a section of one of the old military runways. There are still hundreds of falling down buildings at this abandoned base. Recently while walking along the beach at Atka, I saw what appeared to be a Pratt & Whitney R-1830 half buried in the sand, an engine that once powered a PBY. Looking at these ruins, I've often wondered what it was like then. It has been a pleasure to get a glimpse of those bygone days through reading the accounts in this book.

Perhaps what most characterized the wartime struggle here was the inhospitable conditions, which proved to be more lethal than the Japanese. For every American plane lost in Combat, six were lost to the weather. The violent storms, rapidly forming dense fogs, the rough water and windy conditions will forever remain the same, as will the inhospitable terrain that surrounds the landing areas. It is difficult to describe what these men were up against. It is difficult to imagine what it must have been like to show up here with limited preparation and set up to conduct operations. These men engaged in a major wartime undertaking in an environment that proved to be more treacherous than their enemy.

The evidence of the war here is fading, as the wind and rain are rapidly reclaiming the timeless Aleutian landscape. The world is gradually enduring the loss of the generation who made the sacrifice to fight on these islands. Soon there will be nothing left. This book documents a human achievement that merits being remembered. It tells a story that is worth reading.

Dutch Harbor, February 2001

Rick Knecht, Director, Museum of the Aleutians

World War II was a conflict so enormous that it is still nearly always referred to by people throughout the world as simply "the war." The Museum of the Aleutians opened its doors in 1999, dedicated to preserving the human heritage of the Aleutian Islands. Our building rests on the concrete of an Army warehouse, once part of Fort Mears. The bunkers, Quonsets, cabanas, and trenches have been part of life in Unalaska and Dutch Harbor for 60 years now. As in many other former battle theatres, the war remains by far the largest turning point in our collective memory. Villages were destroyed, Aleut peoples interned, and ancient lifeways suddenly cut short forever. Entire islands were transformed by military construction, leaving behind roads, airstrips, and buildings that even today form much of the infrastructure of Aleutian Island communities.

This book is not about warring nations but the experience of ordinary individuals, transformed by extraordinary events. Tens of thousands of men and women became part of our lives during the war years, and the Aleutians became part of theirs. We are grateful to Jeff Dickrell for letting the men of Patrol Wing Four speak for themselves in this book. Their tales are quietly told, but are filled with the power and eloquence of authentic experience. We are proud to begin our publication series with the publication of *Center of the Storm*.

TABLE OF CONTENTS

NAVY PATROL BOMBER
THE PBY

In the days before radar and satellites, the Navy could only see as far as their eyes allowed. If an enemy was just over the horizon, they would remain undetected. In order to extend the range of their vision, the Navy developed patrol planes. It was assumed that Navy planes would never need to operate from a land base, so patrol planes were flying boats: planes that had a boat–like hull. Large ships were equipped with their own single–engine, float monoplanes. They would be launched from the deck, land on the water and be retrieved by crane.

For long distance patrolling, the Navy relied on a twin–engine, long–range flying boat, the PBY. (Patrol Bomber, the "Y" showed the plane was built by the company Consolidated) They were known to their crews as P-boats, Yoke boats or Catalinas. Special ships called Seaplane Tenders were created to supply the P-boats with food, fuel and bombs. This allowed the PBY squadrons to operate out of bays far beyond established bases.

Vern Monckton VP-41

When I joined VP-41 our aircraft were Catalina Flying Boats (PBY–5) which were designed to operate off of water and did not have landing gear. The aircraft were either tied to buoys or anchored when not flying. A small crew was kept on board when the aircraft was on the water. Special ships known as Seaplane Tenders (The USS Williamson, Gillis and Casco) were as-

signed to Patrol Air Wing Four (PatWing-4) for support during advance operations. This included providing living quarters and food for squadron personnel also fuel and supplies for the aircraft. If the engines required maintenance, special platforms were attached to the engine cowling to work from. Many tools went to the ocean bottom during these operations.

A PBY refueling off the stern of the USS *Williamson*. These converted destroyers had no special setup for servicing the planes. Men use long bamboo poles to hold the PBY away from the ship. The red dot in the center of the star was discontinued in May 1942.

CREW POSITIONS

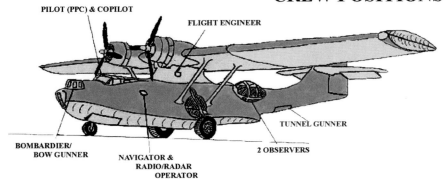

PILOT (PPC) & COPILOT

FLIGHT ENGINEER

BOMBARDIER/
BOW GUNNER

NAVIGATOR &
RADIO/RADAR
OPERATOR

2 OBSERVERS

TUNNEL GUNNER

The crew required a minimum of seven: Pilot, Copilot, Navigator, Radioman, Flight Engineer and two observers in the blisters. Aleutian flying required some extra personnel and positions.

Bob Larson VP-41

Essentially, we had at least two people for each position. Since our patrols were quite long we could spell each other off during the flight and take rest periods. In addition to flight instruction, the Navy gave all pilots some training in navigation, radio code, seamanship, gunnery, and bombsight operation. Theoretically, a pilot could be expected to man any station in the PBY. We had a PPC (patrol plane commander) and three other pilots who rotated between copilot, navigator, and bombardier/turret gunner.

We had two radio/radar men who took turns at the radio. We also had two machinists mates who manned the engineer's station in the wing filet. We also had two ordnancemen who took care of arming the ship and usually manned the waist guns.

During battle stations we had one pilot at the turret gun, two pilots in the cockpit and one at the navigation table. One radioman was at the radio/radar station. One mech. was at the engineer's station and one was usually manning the "tunnel gun" which stuck out of a lower hatchway aft. With the waist guns being manned by the ordnancemen, this left one person as a kind of reserve.

A PBY with a bone in her teeth. PBYs were considered "flying boats" as opposed to "float planes," because they floated on their fuselage instead of pontoons.

This would be a great flying day in the Aleutians. Clear weather, low wind and a landfall in sight. The crews of PatWing-4 knew every rock and point up and down the chain. This was the most reliable method of navigation.

A flight engineer peers from his tower under the wing.
PHOTO VIA H. FORT.

Since I really liked to navigate and the other pilots did not, I usually ended up at the navigation table. Bill did rotate us among the different positions, so we could get experienced at each station.

Lloyd Black VP-41

I joined VP-41 July 15th, 1942. Assigned duty as navigator to Stewart's crew. In those days all navigators were pilots. The Navy had not started the "navigator only" designation.

On a rare sunny day the full crew of a PBY swarms over the nose of the plane.

Comedian Joe E. Brown learns to navigate a PBY.

All Navy pilots were dead reckoning, relative motion, radio, celestial and Loran qualified navigators. In early squadrons you first served as a navigator, then elevated to copilot. After 500 hours experience you were sent to OTU (operational training unit) to qualify for PPC.

One of the most important positions on the PBY was navigator. In 1942, in the Aleutians, there were no navigational aids, only three airfields and atrocious weather. Location was done by "dead reckoning." That is—the navigator sat at a table with a speed indicator, compass and stopwatch. With these he was supposed to be able to follow the plane's course on the map and navigate. This was fine in calm weather, but when wind pushed the plane off its heading, it could screw things up. Wind direction and speed had to be estimated in the air.

Bob Larson VP-41

A navigator at work plotting a course. With no electronic aids, navigation in the Aleutians usually relied on "dead reckoning," using time course and speed.
PHOTO VIA H.H. FORT

There were generally three ways we could estimate wind direction and speed. We could take a drift sight with the bombsight or with a regular gyro stabilized drift sight on some airplanes. If you took drift angles on two or more headings, you could work a vector solution on the Mk III plotting board and get and answer.

We also got reasonably proficient at estimating the wind speed and direction from the state of the sea. You had to be flying pretty close to the water for that method to be accurate enough. However, we did spend a lot of time under 1,000 ft of altitude, where that method would apply well. At night we had a way of determining drift angle by using a smoke float. We carried smoke floats, which could be thrown out the tunnel hatch. When it hit the water a flame would be ignited and you could track it as it receded. The angle between the airplane heading and the location of the smoke float light would yield a drift angle. When you repeated the maneuver at another heading you had enough information to calculate the wind direction and velocity on the Mk III plotter. About sunshots—we made our observations at the gun blisters, usually with the doors open. Occasionally I would take one from the copilot's seat. We had aircraft octants with artificial horizons, essentially a very sensitive bubble. Since the bubble was affected by airplane motion, we took sights over a two–minute period and averaged out the readings. The PBY was always "Dutch Rolling," that is, the nose would be slowly oscillating from right to left and back, which affected the sights. Aircraft celestial shots were not as accurate as shipboard shots because of the motion effect. A "good" aircraft shot might have a five–mile error. A "bad" shot could have a 25–mile error in it. However, since visibility from an airplane is a lot better than from a ship, we could live with these inaccuracies. Incidentally, an octant measured the angular distance from the horizon to the celestial body, yielding "altitude," in degrees (not to be confused with airplane altitude in feet). Azimuths were not measured. They were part of the calculation, using an assumed position. (You can tell I was a former instructor in celestial navigation).

They were also equipped with the first airborne radars in the Navy. The squadrons had been operating in the Aleutians for years but only flying in optimal weather. Wing Commander Geheres realized that it would be impossible to operate on a war footing without radar.

The Radioman doubled up, working the rudimentary radar system. The PBYs of Patwing-4 had the first airborne radar in the Navy, a necessity in the Aleutians. PHOTO VIA H.H. FORT

Lloyd Black VP-41

There were no radio–ranges or homing devices in 1942. Radar was the old APS 15. No images, just return blips indicating distance and direction. It took a very good Radio–Radar operator to tune in and interpret the small radar screen. Flying low over the water produced a "gross return" making it difficult to read.

Bill Thies VP-41

As to the procedure for coming in—you touched on one of my favorite stories. VP-41 had the first airborne radar installations. I think Geheres (bless his heart) saw to it that PatWing-4 would get it before any other squadron in the en-

6

All communication was via Morse code, using a telegraph key.
PHOTO VIA P. BUCHANAN

This PBY crashed on the flanks of Mt. Makushin, ten miles northwest of Dutch Harbor. There was one survivor.

Two crewman sit in the watertight door between compartments inside a PBY.
PHOTO VIA B. BUCHANNAN.

tire Navy. It was crude being the first ever manufactured for aircraft. I don't really remember the range, maybe ten miles. I don't think altitude made any difference. The only problem was, the generators could not carry the load of both the radio transmitter and the radar at the same time. To send a radio message, we had to turn off the radar.

Standing orders were when we were returning to Dutch, when we reached some point (I forget its name) we must send an "IN" report and ID. When I was coming in the rain and fog I NEEDED that radar, so I didn't turn it off to send the damn IN report. Consequently, when Dutch radar picked up an aircraft that hadn't sent an IN report and not identified itself, the Army went to alert and manned all the guns.

I don't remember how many times Foley (our CO) threatened to court martial me if I didn't send an "IN" report. Of course he was catching hell from some Army colonel or General in charge of the Dutch troops who was also bitching to Gehres. But I owe my life to the radar helping me fly blind through the mountains and passages on the way in.

Needless to say the CO just threw up his hands and gave up! I forget how many of my friends crashed on the mountains around Dutch shortly after they had sent their "IN" report. I never used the runway they built at Dutch. Too short. Maybe some of the guys did, but I preferred the water.

One major problem with taking a driftsight from the rear of the PBY was that a "pee tube" was located directly in front of the sight. Using this covered the scope with a soon frozen spray. Since PBYs were expected to be in the air for up to and beyond 12–hour patrols certain necessities were aboard. In the center compartment was a small two–burner stove. There were also a couple of bunks and in the rear a rudimentary toilet.

Bill Thies VP-41

In front of each pilot's seat was a "Pee–tube" so that the pilot could relieve himself without leaving his post.

Lloyd Black VP-41

In the aft last compartment, aft of the blister section, was a metal can with a liner for BM toilet necessity. To take a leak, there was a large funnel with a rubber tube through the tail section bottom. As you went, the urine would be sucked out through the tube by a vacuum created by the aircraft slip-stream. One cold day I started to take a leak. It ran all over my pants and boots. The urine from a previous user had fro-zen almost immediately it was so cold. Cold piss frozen on your clothes is not the best of times. So go the sagas of flying in the Aleutians.

The PBY was expected to remain aloft for 12–hour patrols, so cooking facilities were needed.
PHOTO VIA B. BUCHANAN

The PBY was never intended for combat, so was extremely under–armed. Up front, in the bow turret was a single .30–cal. machine gun. It was matched by a .30–cal. that stuck out the bottom of the plane through a hatch in the tail. One crawled down a tunnel to get to this position. The .30–caliber gun was considered a "popgun" against other airplanes. On each side, in the blister, was a heavy .50–caliber machine gun that had a very wide angle of fire. But operating with the blisters open slowed the plane down and made the interior almost unbearably cold.

There were many blind spots on the PBY that an enemy could take advantage of, especially directly behind. The tunnel gun could only fire downwards, the blisters could not fire straight

A front view (left)of the PBY showing the cockpit area and the bow turret, and rear view (right) of the PBY showing the location of the observation blisters.

back without hitting the tail. When attacked, a good pilot would weave the plane in order to allow the blister gunners to get a clear shot.

The PBY was technically a "patrol bomber" but its payload was very small. There were three weapons the PBY could carry under it's wings: Four 500–lb. GP (General Purpose) bombs or four Mk.17 Depth Bombs (for use against submarines) or Two 2,000–lb. torpedoes. Often a combina-

At right, the bow turret of a PBY. It contained a Norden bombsight and a .30–cal. machine gun.

Below, a crewman firing the "tunnel gun," a .30–cal. machine gun, which stuck out of a hole in the tail section. PHOTO VIA H. FORT.

The observation blisters contained flexible .50 cal. machine guns. These were the main defensive armament of the PBY. PHOTO VIA H. FORT.

Al Knack sits, bundled up, in the blister area of a PBY. The main job of the PBY was observation and the blisters provided an excellent view of the Aleutians. PHOTO VIA AL KNACK.

Above, an outside view of the blister on a PBY showing the .50 cal. machine gun. PHOTO VIA H. FORT. Right, standard armament for the PBYs was either depth bombs (left) or General Purpose (GP) bombs, ranging in weight from 250 lbs. (shown here), 500 lbs. (common) to 1,000 lbs. One–ton torpedoes were also carried—with much difficulty— on occasion.

tion was used of a torpedo on one wing, two GPs on the other. Using a PBY to deliver a torpedo was risky business. The torpedo was very heavy, and the low, slow approach need to launch a torpedo was death in such a lumbering plane.

Bob Larson VP-41

If we were loaded with 500–lb. bombs, there was a bombardier trained on the Norden bomb-sight who manned the forward turret, but the sight which was designed to work best at 10,000 feet, was never used. That is why we reverted to "glide" bombing, because rarely did we ever get above 1,000 feet up there.

Flying in the Aleutians in the summer of 1942 was about the worst situation a crew could experience. In addition to difficulties with weather, facilities and navigation, it was cold, even in the summer. Crews often watched water freeze in the bilges soon after they were airborne, coffee froze in insulated bottles and heaters for the crew were non–existent.

Bill Thies VP-41

We wore the lightweight flight jackets to roam around on the ground when it was not too cold. I don't remember a time when we were not wearing the very heavy and bulky leather fleece lined jackets and pants when in the air. (VERY difficult to use the "P" tube under the pilots seat !)

Bob Larson VP-41

In the summertime we usually wore the standard cotton flight suit over Army issue trousers. Over that the standard goatskin intermediate jacket or the winter fleece jacket. Over that the life jacket and parachute harness, which was the quick attachable chest chute type. We usually wore shoepacs, with leather uppers and rubber lowers, which were good for tramping around the tundra. In wintertime we would add long johns, perhaps a jersey-lined pants, and what-ever, lined, flight suit we could lay our hands on.

Later in the war we got down–filled jackets and pants, which were warm and light. I never did care much for the fleece flight pants because of their bulk and stiffness. We seldom wore our uniforms unless there was some special occasion. Otherwise our clothes were a mixture of whatever the Navy or the Army had available. I had an overweight copilot one time who wore so much clothing in winter that he would get stuck in the seat, which was none too large. We also liked the Army billed cap, because it shielded your eyes for those occasional times that you could see the sun.

The PBY-5 was designed to operate on water. In order to get the P-boat on land a complicated procedure was employed. When the PBY-5A with retractable landing gear was issued in April of 1942 beaching planes became a much easier ordeal.

Vern Monckton VP-41

When the PBY-5 aircraft operated from Naval Air Stations, special wheel mounts were attached to them so that they could be brought on land. My first experience around the aircraft was when I was assigned to the Beach Crew. This was exciting, as it was the duty of the Beach Crew to safely get the flying boats from land into the water (launched) and from the water back onto land (beached).

The members of the Beach Crew that had to enter the water wore heavy rubber suits that fastened tightly about the neck. These suits were only slight protection against the

PBY-5s had no landing gear; they were simply tied to buoys. When they needed to be hauled out, wheels were attached in the water. It could be a cold experience. Kodiak N.A.S. 1942.

A PBY approaching the ramp at Dutch Harbor. The PPC had to turn the plane 180° after landing to get the rear of the PBY facing the ramp. Note the two men acting as counter balances on the wingtip, so that the opposite wing float would clear the ramp.

A PBY-5A gets wheels attached on the ramp at Dutch Harbor.

Once the wheels were attached a tractor would pull the plane out of the water. N.A.S. Dutch Harbor. Note the two men on the wing and in the water.
PHOTO VIA PATWING-4 COLLECTION

The PBY-5A could simply drive up the ramp on its own landing gear. N.A.S. Dutch Harbor.
PHOTO VIA UNALASKA CITY SCHOOL COLLECTION.

frigid water of the Aleutians, however. When removing or installing the mounts the men were in water up to their chest or neck. Launching and beaching involved a coordinated effort by both the flight crew and the beach crew.

During launching the aircraft engines were used to provide forward motion while the beach crew assisted in controlling direction and a rope between the tail of the plane and a tractor controlled forward motion. Once the aircraft was safely in the water, the side mounts and tail mount were removed from the aircraft.

Beaching was a much more involved operation, as it required expert co–operation between the beach crew under the Beach Master and the aircrew under the Patrol Plane Commander. The aircraft was taxied toward the ramp and turned so that one wing tip float passed near enough to the Beach Crew for a line to be attached to the float, and as the plane continued to turn the tail came near enough for another line to be attached to the tail. By controlling these two lines from the beach and the pilot controlling the engines the aircraft was positioned so that the two side mounts and tail mount could be attached to the hull of the plane. The side mount tires contained enough antifreeze to provide only slight positive buoyancy so that after the upper lock pin was in place the mount could be forced under water and the lower lock pins could be put in place. When the mounts were locked in place, the tractor would tow the aircraft up the ramp and to the parking area or the hangar.

When war was declared, the only Naval Air Stations in Alaska were in Sitka and Kodiak. Dutch Harbor was barely operational as a facility. Because of this, coupled with six months of the massive Japanese offensive, orders were not by the book.

Robert Donley VP-42

Prior to the attack on Dutch all orders were given formally in writing. When one was sent to a place other than where the squadron was stationed, orders were given as, "You are hereby detached and will report to…" etc. After the attack on Dutch there were no more orders in writing unless one was ordered back to the States.

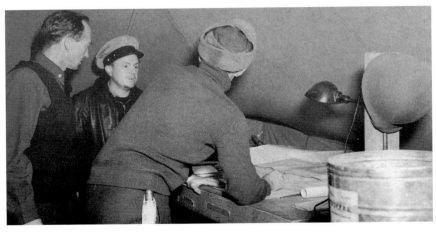

Top, VP-42 operated out of a tent at Cold Bay. On the far left is Lt. Comdr. James Russell, unit C.O. Bottom, the Operations Hut in Dutch Harbor, June 1942. On the left is Lt. Peter "the fox" Boyle, X.O. Next to him is Lt. Cmdr. Paul Foley, commander VP-41 and PPC John Herron. Herron was later lost. Foley commanded groups at Dutch and Umnak airfield, 50 miles to the west.

Bill Thies VP-41

"Operations" planned the flights, what sectors who was going to fly in, insuring planes were ready to fly, etc. They were probably the most busy of any of the squadrons different divisions.

As "lowly" pilots, we were never involved in the paper work of Operations, Orders, etc. There were never any written orders or instructions. We were told our mission by the C.O. or Operations Officer, either to individual PPCs or sometimes to a group of PPCs.

Check out of the plane by the PPC was cursory. We had such good maintenance crews, we trusted them implicitly to make sure all was OK. The other thing, the enlisted flight engineer, who was responsible for the planes readiness, always flew on the mission, so it was his neck too, if something went wrong!

There isn't much else, we just listened (we being the PPC, the copilots and navigator) to what the old man had to say, went to the plane, signed off on a "yellow sheet" which was something that went into maintenance files, got in the plane, started the engines and took off.

There was no A.T.C. (Air Traffic Control) as such. There was some sort of a structure (Just a hut. We called it the radio shack.) from which some radio operators could see the bay, and gave clearance to enter the air space, but the PPC just floated the PBY and took off when he darn well felt like it.

Lloyd Black VP-41

My recalls are about an island shrouded in fog, williwaws screaming down the mountain side flipping the PBYs into vertical flight attitude. So many times it was necessary to sneak into the harbor 50 feet over the water surface with the wing surfaces rubbing the overcast. It took skills to set the PBY down in the water inside the sand spit. The water area was so limited it was necessary to take off with a gas load at minimal, skim the ocean's surface, suddenly there was Umnak jumping out of the fog. Umnak was our refuge to land and take on a full load of gasoline, approximately 1,475 gallons.

Many times we arrived in the late afternoon to Umnak, fueled up, ate dinner/breakfast in the Army Engineer's Mess in order to utilize time for a patrol all the way down the Chain past Kiska, Shemya and on to occupied Attu. I remember the engineering of cutting the side off of Ballyhoo, by the SeaBees, to construct a runway. On takeoff and landing the wing facing the mountain had marginal distance to the rock face. The PBY wing span was 104 feet. We used the runway with light loads, takeoff and approach weather negate instrument conditions.

Rob Donley VP-42

One of the problems in taking off from the harbor at Dutch was the spit. We took off going out the harbor entrance and it was necessary to start as far back in the Harbor as we could in order to clear the spit.

A PBY lands just outside the spit, which creates Dutch Harbor. The N.A.S. is off to the right.
PHOTO VIA MUSEUM OF THE ALEUTIANS, DRAKE COLLECTION

Ensign Frederick Andrew Smith crashed on the spit early in 1942. We called him Andy. He started a takeoff with ice on his wings, and as he approached the spit, realizing he didn't have flying speed, he attempted to hop the spit by pulling the plane off the water. He landed in the middle of the spit and burned. I was given the dubious honor of escorting his body back to his wife who lived in Pensacola, Florida. It was a long and arduous journey as transportation was by train in those days.

14

PPC Smith tried to take off inside the spit and crashed on it, all hands were lost. May 1942.

N.A.S. Sand Point on Lake Washington outside Seattle. This was the main base of the Wing before the war.
PHOTO VIA ED FROEHLICH

PATROL WING FOUR BEFORE THE STORM
SQUADRONS VP-41 AND VP-42

Patrol Wing Four was composed of five squadrons (VP-41-45) of 12 PBYs each. The "V" designated that the squadron flew "heavier–than–air" craft as opposed to blimps and dirigibles. The "P" stood for patrol. VP-41 and -42 were assigned to Sand Point NAS (Naval Air Station) located outside Seattle on Lake Washington before the war. Starting in the late 1930s the Navy was establishing a seaplane base in Sitka. During the summer months each squadron, alternately, would fly to southeast Alaska and sometimes to the Aleutians. It was believed that PBYs could not operate in Alaska in the winter. Seaplane Tenders would sail along to service the P-boats. Patrols occasionally went as far out as Kiska.

The PBYs were not painted but left with a natural metal finish. There was no reason to camouflage American planes. Not until December 1940 were patrol planes painted with blue–gray upper surfaces and light gray beneath. Prior to it designation as VP-41, it was VP-16 (VP-42 was VP-17). The planes had natural metal topside with black anti–fouling paint on the bottom. Tails were gaudily painted for quick identification.

Most of the men serving in the highly technical aviation units were not draftees but experienced men, familiar with their machines.

Off Front Beach, Unalaska/Dutch Harbor. A small boat tows the plane to its moorage.

Above, a 1939 deployment to Dutch Harbor. The flat area beyond Margaret Bay is the future site of Ft. Mears.
PHOTO VIA PATWING-4 COLLECTION

Left, tails of VP-16 were gaudily painted for easy identification.
PHOTO VIA ED FROEHLICH

Near right, prior to VP-41 it was VP-16. The planes were not painted but did have anti–fouling coating below the waterline. In front of the numbers was the squadron emblem, a wolf and firtree. From an 1939 deployment to Sitka.
PHOTO VIA ED FROEHLICH

Far right, before it was VP-42 it was VP-17. Note natural finish and tail design. Somewhere over the Alaskan coast. PBYs were painted in the light blue upper, gray lower scheme beginning in 1941.

PatWing pilots J. Jonson, P. Foley and J. Raven confer with a station officer at Dutch Harbor, 1941. Both Jonson and Raven were killed in plane crashes in 1942.

Bill Thies VP-4

Most of the guys were in the Navy before the war, but not all. Most of the enlisted men were old timers. The senior (Full Lt. and above) officers were old timers and all Naval Academy. The Ensigns and Junior Grades (JGs), like myself, came in about 1938 and 1939.

Bob Biddle VP-42

To start with, I joined VP-42 in October 1941 coming from the old USS Saratoga *that went into dry dock for repairs at Bremerton. I was sent to Sand Point NAS, Seattle for further transfer to the USS* Gillis, *an old four–stack destroyer that had been converted to a sea plane tender, servicing VP-41 and 42. While in Sand Point the yeoman in personnel asked if anyone wanted to volunteer for Patrol Sqd. 42. Out of 28 of us I was the only one who said "Aye." That started my association with PatWing Four's finest squadron VP-42.*

A PBY-5 of VP-41 on a 1941 deployment to the brand new facility at Dutch Harbor. PHOTOS VIA JIM FOLEY

18

A PBY-5 of VP-41 at Dutch Harbor, 1941. PHOTOS VIA JIM FOLEY

Bill Thies VP-41

I had joined VP-41 in 1940 after completing a three–year tour with another PBY squadron in San Diego. I was a qualified Patrol Plane Commander (PPC) and had been the Master Bomber for formation drops. VP-41s home base was Seattle, but we didn't see it very often. We were in Kodiak on December 7, 1941 when Pearl Harbor was attacked. We had been flying long sector searches each day for several weeks before the attack. So had the Hawaii PBY Squadrons.

In February 1942 we moved to Tongue Point, Oregon near the mouth of the Columbia River. We expanded from a six–plane to a 12-plane squadron, with new PBY-5A aircraft equipped with radar. We received and trained a lot of new pilots and crews, and a group of newly gradu-ated ground officers from Officer Candidate School (the so–called 90–day wonders). They were excellent people from all walks of civilian life, and they took over most of the administrative duties normally assigned to the pilots.

Our next destination was a well kept secret. Our new skipper, LCDR. Paul Foley, did leak word to pack our white uniforms, so we expected to go to a warm climate. When we arrived in Dutch Harbor instead in May 1942, many men had very little cold weather clothing. After the Jap attack on June 3, before the dust had hardly settled, one of our new ground officers, En. Tex Smyer commandeered a truck and visited the Army Supply building, which had been hit in the attack. He returned with a load of wool socks, mittens, underwear, etc., which he distrib-uted to the needy. The Skipper was impressed with the young man's initiative and fast re-sponse. He appointed him Officer–in–Charge of VP-41 Detachment, and sent him to Umnak with Dutch Schultz and a small maintenance crew. Keith Wheeler (news correspondent) when he arrived, was equally impressed with Tex. He wrotep) a loving report of the "Hotel de Smyer" in his book The Pacific was My Beat.

Vern Monckton VP-41

I arrived at the Naval Air Station, Kodiak, Alaska for assignment to Patrol Squadron Forty–One (VP-41) in October 1941 after graduation from Aviation Machinist School in Chicago, Illinois and Recruit Training in San Diego, California. Transportation from Seattle to Kodiak was aboard the USS Grant, *which was a German passenger ship that had been captured during World War I and served as a troop carrier. Accommodations were less than pleasant. I was sick from the time the ship cleared Puget Sound until it docked in Kodiak.*

Entering the Navy in Colorado, I had very little knowledge of the Navy or what was expected of me other than to do whatever I was told. I was assigned to compartment cleaning, mess cooking and other menial tasks for the first month before I was allowed in the hangar area where the aircraft were located.

VP-16 PBYs at NAS Kodiak before the war. Not much space for rapid deployment. PHOTO VIA ED FROEHLICH

Ed Froehlich VP-41

I enlisted in the Navy in Des Moines, Iowa January 1932. I reported to VP-16 (Later VP-41) at Sand Point, Washington for duty as AMM 1/C in June of 1938. Having previous flying boat experience (PH-1) in VP-8 Pearl Harbor, Hawaii, 1933-35. I was soon qualified as a PBY Plane Captain (PC) and Flight Engineer (FE). Prior to the Pearl Harbor attack I was assigned P.C. and F.E. for the X.O. then the C.O., but I flew with all of VP-41 pilots at various times. In March 1942 I was P.C. for Lt. Chuck Reimanns flying black takeoffs on patrol out of Tongue Point, Oregon. I missed flying one weekend for business in Seattle, and Mr. Reimanns' plane and crew were lost in an instrument takeoff, crashed in the river. All of the crew's bodies were recovered down river near Astoria except Crump's AMM 2/C who relieved me as Plane Captain.

In late May '42 the squadron flew to Dutch Harbor when the possible attack by the Japs became known. On arriving at Dutch Harbor we were assigned to combat crews. I was assigned to crew "E" consisting of PPC Lt. Jim Bowers; copilot Lt. Jg SH Dinsmore; 2nd copilot and navigator Lt. Jg. Brad Reynolds; PC & FE ACMM Froehlich; 2nd AMM 2/C Ainscough; 1st Radioman ACR Sissenwood; 2nd Radioman AR 3/C Greene; and a 3/C AMM and a 3/C AOM, a nine man crew.

On December 7, 1941 the Japanese bombed Pearl Harbor, Hawaii. It was the main Naval base in the pacific. Using aircraft carriers the Japanese were able to launch devastating attacks from the air, never before thought possible. The military was in a near panic. If the Japanese could get so close to Hawaii and attack without being detected, they could be anywhere.

Because of tensions with Japan, VP-41 was already stationed in Alaska, based out of Kodiak on December 7th. VP-42 was operating out of Tongue Point, Oregon at the mouth of the Columbia River. In January 1942, the squadrons flew down to San Diego and received 12 new PBY-5A amphibious planes, doubling the squadron's size. Then VP-41 rotated positions with VP-42 heading to Kodiak, Alaska. The men of PatWing Four were anxious that the Japanese were headed their way. The serious business of war was new to them and mistakes were made.

Bill Thies VP-41

When we got news of Pearl Harbor, VP-41 was in Kodiak. My wife was with me and most of the married personnel had their wives up there, too.

A J4F "Duck" lands at Dutch Harbor. The airstrip was not completed until after the bombing.

We were immediately sent out on patrol to the south with two PBYs per sector. I was out from Kodiak about 200 or 300 miles when we sighted a ship making high speed on a northerly course. When I put my binoculars on it, it was the BIGGEST ship I had ever seen. We were at an altitude of probably 2 or 3,000 feet. I sent a contact report to Kodiak, that a Japanese Battle Cruiser was steaming towards Kodiak at 35 knots!

Of course, Kodiak went on full alert, the Army manned all the guns, and all the women and children were sent to the power house for shelter. Shortly thereafter, a Duck (Navy float plane) crashed in Woman's Bay. It came in for a landing on the water but had put his wheels down, and proceeded to sink. He had been out on patrol, so those on shore thought he had been hit by AA fire.

I radioed my wingman that I was going to 10,000 feet and bomb the ship. I had the very best bombardier aboard, a Chief Petty Officer (Ordnance). He never missed on practice runs. We had four 500-lb. bombs. My wingman was an Ensign who was a Naval Academy graduate (I was an Ensign, too) and of course, he knew his ships. His name was Jep Johnson. The wingtip floats on Jep's PBY would not retract, so he could not get to altitude to make a bomb run. (Why we ALWAYS practiced drops from 10,000 feet I never figured out.) He radioed back that he would remain at low altitude and observe the results of the bombing. On the way up I kept sending coded radio messages on U.S. frequencies that the ship, if it were friendly, could identify itself. I also kept flashing the Aldis lamp with visible messages, so the ship could answer if it were friendly. No response, so we started on our run. The ship started zigzagging and picked up more speed. We had about a minute to go before the drop when Jep, in an excited urgent voice came over my radio, and I will never forget his exact words, "BILL, BILL, DON'T DROP – THE SHIP IS A UNITED STATES DESTROYER!!!"

Needless to say, I was embarrassed and thought, "Boy am I going to catch hell for this." I banked away and told the radioman to send a "Z" message to Kodiak. Z messages were made up of three letters starting with Z, i.e. ZIP and you would look in the decode book and ZIP meant "Ignore my last message," which is what I sent. Well, when Kodiak got that, they thought the Japanese had sent it for a trick. So they sent me—What is PPC's nickname? I sent back— "Bill." Then Kodiak in all its wisdom decided that the Japanese knew that most Americans were called Bill. So Kodiak sent—What is PPC's middle name? There is not another "Nouris" in the world that I ever heard of, and when Kodiak got that they knew I had sent an authentic "Z" message.

The Army stood down, and the women and kids went back to their apartments. When I returned, Gehres had me on the carpet. The only thing that came of it was a lot of extra study on ship identification.

Sequel: When the destroyer anchored, Lt.Cdr. Norm Garton, the CO, got hold of me and over lots of martinis, told me he was scared to death because he was aware that it was a VP-41 PBY and knew of our reputation for accurate bombing. The destroyer was the USS Gillis, a seaplane tender that we had worked with before. When he left Pearl Harbor in a big rush, they forgot to load the latest identification codes and that is why what he was returning in answer to my inquiries were not correct, which only aroused my suspicions that he was an enemy.

Point for operations and training with the new PBY-5A aircraft. During this time, I was assigned to the bombsight shop. I have no idea what prompted this decision, as I was qualified to be rated as an Aviation Machinist Mate Third Class. The following month I received a rate of Aviation Ordinanceman Third Class, which didn't make the Chief Ordinanceman very happy because it took one of his billets. The reason for the Ordinanceman rate was that there was no rate for those working on bombsights because it was so highly classified at that time.*

When December 7 came we headed for Tongue Point, Oregon for patrol duties. It was there in January that my best buddy, a lad named Bob Wallenstien learned his brother was killed on the USS Arizona at Pearl Harbor. Sad times were had. Shortly thereafter, I was sent to Fleet Torpedo School in San Diego. After finishing school it was back to VP-42, located at N.A.S. Kodiak. VP-42 was going to carry the MK 23 torpedo on the PBYs. A scary thought on a plane so slow and cumbersome.

Frank Moy VP-41

We were in Kodiak on December 7th, 1941. Three PBYs were sent to Dutch Harbor, so we spent Christmas 1941 in Dutch Harbor where we lived in civilian houses. We spent 22 months in that area. We each had one beer with our meal, as a special treat.

Jim Edmundson VP-41

I entered the Navy on the 28th day of December 1941 and ended up in VP-41 at Dutch three days prior to the Japs bombing there.

Ralph Erskine VP-41

When we arrived in Dutch Harbor from Seattle on 1 June, 1942 one of the first things that I did was go to the Naval Supply Depot to draw some trailing wire for our antennas and found that they just had 3,000 feet. Each airplane used 500 feet on the trailing wire antenna for low frequency transmission, so we could see that the Depot did not have this and other supplies necessary to keep the PBYs flying. But we did keep them flying because our maintenance officers and Chiefs had foresight to bring along enough spares and tools to operate 15 PBYs for three months in an advanced base operation.

Ralph Erskine VP-41 (journal entry)

2 June 1942. We got up at 0400 for general quarters as we expected the Japanese to attack us. There were no ammunition for us, so we should have stayed in bed. The ammunition ship arrived later in the morning, and the soldiers worked all day and most of the night to unload the ship.

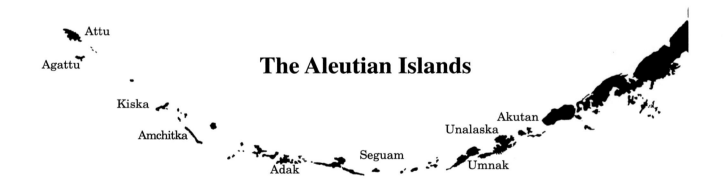

The Aleutian Islands

THE ALEUTIAN BASES
SUMMER 1942

In June 1942 there were exactly three military bases to defend the Aleutians: Cold Bay on the Alaska Peninsula, Dutch Harbor on Unalaska Island and 60 miles away the airfield on Umnak Island. PatWing-4 was split up between the three. Capt. James Russell, based in Cold Bay commanded the PBYs of VP-42. Based at Dutch Harbor, the planes of VP-41, commanded by Capt. Paul Foley were split between there and Umnak. In command of the Wing was Commodore Leslie Gehres in Kodiak. There were also provisional bases at Akutan 40 miles east of Dutch and Sand Point, a cannery town just outside Cold Bay.

DUTCH HARBOR:
NAVAL OPERATING BASE, NAVAL AIR STATION
FT. MEARS: ARMY POST

The main base west of Kodiak, Dutch Harbor was planned as the furthest west American base. Built on top of an old Gold Rush shipping town, the Navy had several facilities on Amaknak Island. The port of Dutch Harbor surrounded the Naval Operating Base (N.O.B.). This served the Navy's ships. A Submarine Base was constructed in the inner harbor. On the edge of the N.O.B., was the Naval Air Station. The N.A.S. was designed to service seaplanes, as there was no room for an airstrip. (One was carved out of the side of Ballyhoo Mountain after the attacks). The Army

An aerial view of the bases at Dutch Harbor. On the narrow neck of land at the foot of Mt. Ballyhoo is the N.A.S. To the right is the Naval Operating Base. The long white buildings are Ft. Mears, the Army base. The Aleut community of Unalaska is out of the picture to the lower right. The mile long spit creates Dutch Harbor.

set up Ft. Mears nearby, to provide defense. Large cannons were placed ringing the harbor and observation outposts were established on outlying points.

When the Japanese bombed Dutch Harbor June 3 and 4, 1942 there were only six PBY patrol planes nearby. Army airfields at Umnak and Cold Bay were established but were of little help. Damage was slight, and Dutch remained the main naval base in the Aleutians until autumn of 1942.

Construction began in July 1940. All military construction was initially located on Amaknak Island across a narrow channel from the village of Unalaska, pop. 300. By September 1941 the base was manned and operational. Because Dutch Harbor was a prewar base it had real buildings with plumbing and beds. At the other bases housing was in tents and Quonset huts, with very few comforts.

Cold Bay: Ft. Randall (Army Airfield)

Built on uninhabited tundra, the airfield at Cold Bay was one of two secret Army Air Force bases in the Aleutians when the Japanese bombed in June 1942. Cold Bay was located on the Alaska Peninsula and had an excellent harbor. Construction began before the war in September 1940 with plans calling for a 5,000–foot paved runway. Construction continued, adding more

On final approach to the strip at Cold Bay.

Created from scratch on the tundra, the airfield at Cold Bay had far less accommodations than Dutch Harbor. A VP-42 PBY sits on a revetment in Cold Bay, May 1942. All maintenance was done outdoors.

runways, until the Army departed in 1944. Also located at Cold Bay was a small Naval Air Station at which was based a squadron of PBY patrol planes. When the Japanese bombed Dutch Harbor there was only a small number of planes located at Cold Bay: 21 P-40 fighters (11th fighter Sqd.)

12 B-26 twin–engine bombers (73rd Bomb. Sqd.)

1 B-24 and 5 B-17 four–engine bombers (36th Bomb. Sqd)

10 PBY Navy patrol planes (VP-42)

P-40s from Cold Bay responded to the attack on June 3rd but arrived after the Japanese had left. Some bombers attacked the enemy fleet but did no damage. When the Japanese were discovered on Kiska, long range bombing missions were launched from Cold Bay.

UMNAK, FT. GLENN (ARMY AIRFIELD)

Located about 60 miles west of the main Naval Base at Dutch Harbor, the secret airfield at Umnak was to provide air cover for the eastern Aleutians. Hacked out of uninhabited tundra, construction of the 5,000–foot runway was begun in January 1942. It was covered with Perfo-

Approaching the strip at Umnak Army Airfield.

Since there was no harbor on Umnak, supplies were transferred from freighter to barge in Chernofski Bay, ten miles away. The barges were simply rammed up on the beach. Note the PBY in the foreground.

rated Steel Planking (a.k.a. Marston matting or P.S.P.) Working 24 hours a day, seven days a week the base was ready by April 5th. The first planes arrived less than two weeks before the attacks on Dutch Harbor. A field expedient, P.S.P. runways sometimes bounced planes 30 feet into the air when landing.

May 1942, a P-40 sits on the Pierced Steel Planking runway at Umnak. This airfield was built to provide fighter cover over Dutch Harbor, 50 miles away. A lack of flat ground prohibited an airstrip there. The spongy tundra sometimes bounced planes 30 feet on landing.

Total air strength on Umnak during the attacks:
12 P-40 fighters (11th & 18th Fighter Sqds.)
6 B-26 twin–engine bombers (77th Bomb. Sqd)
6 PBY Navy Patrol Planes (VP-41)

On June 3rd and 4th, 1942 communications failed and the base at Umnak was never alerted to the attacks on Dutch. However, U.S. fighters jumped Japanese planes returning to their carriers June 4th. Two P-40s were lost as well as four Japanese planes. Missions to Kiska were based from Umnak all summer. Offensive operations moved to Adak in September 1942.

THE DEFENSE OF THE BASES

A 155mm cannon emplacement in Dutch Harbor. A battery of four of these guns provided the main defense against seaborne invasion. They were mounted on platforms, which allowed a 360° rotation.

While the defense of the Aleutians was the responsibility of the Navy, the defense of their bases from air and ground attack fell to the U.S. Army. To this end, the Army sent three types of units to the Aleutian bases: coastal artillery, antiaircraft artillery and infantry regiments.

Many of these were National Guard units from the Deep South and California. They had been absorbed into the regular Army when tensions with Japan intensified in 1940. In addition to the Army units the Navy also placed several antiaircraft guns around the air station.

A battery of 155mm cannons also protected Umnak Airfield.

The main threat to the Aleutian bases was sea–borne invasion. In the 100 days following the Pearl Harbor attack, the Japanese had struck from the sea and air, occupying most of the South Pacific. They seemed to appear out of nowhere and were invincible.

To defend against such an invasion the Army placed batteries of four 155 mm cannons at the entrances to base harbors. With a range of some 15 miles, they were supposed to destroy an invasion fleet far out to sea. Each gun was able to rotate 360° to cover overland "backdoors." In addition to the big guns, many smaller pieces covered strategic areas.

The defenders of the Aleutians feared a carrier based air attack. This was something new in warfare, perfected by the Japanese. To counter attacks from aircraft the military divided the sky into three layers and classified their weapons accordingly:

High level 10,000 ft.	3–inch gun
Middle level 5,000 ft.	37mm gun
Low Level below 5,000 ft	.50 cal. machine gun

The Navy also added their 20mm and .50–caliber machine guns to the low level defenses.

In 1942 one had to see targets in order to fire effectively. For this reason outposts were situated on outlying points. In order to locate targets at night, enormous spotlights ringed the bay. They were for use against enemy shipping as well as aircraft. Radar was in its infancy at this point. Mountains around Dutch Harbor further limited its use. On board ships, however, it was very effective. In fact, it was the radar aboard the seaplane tender USS *Gillis* that sounded the first warning of enemy planes approaching Dutch Harbor on June 3rd.

Unfortunately, most of the antiaircraft fire over Dutch was ineffective, for two reasons: The crews had never fired live ammunition at a moving target. Secondly, the Japanese planes were too fast for the AA guns to track. These were prewar guns designed to follow older, slower craft. In response to this ineffectiveness, an antiaircraft training school was set up.

In the two attacks only one Japanese plane was shot down by AA fire. A Zero fighter hit by a .50 caliber round in its oil line, crashed on nearby Akutan Island. It was recovered, repaired and flown again. Until then, the U.S. military could not believe enemy planes flew so fast.

The principle heavy antiaircraft weapon used by the U.S. was the 3-inch gun. (File photo)

A 3-inch AA position at Dutch Harbor.

Soldiers man a .50–caliber machine gun high on the slopes of Mt. Ballyhoo above Dutch Harbor.
PHOTO VIA M.O.A. BLOOM COLLECTION

A Navy 20mm AA gun sits, manned, alongside the strip in Cold Bay.

A view of the business end of a well emplaced 20mm AA gun, Dutch Harbor.
PHOTO VIA M.O.A. BLOOM COLLECTION

In order to identify targets at night, huge searchlights were placed in the mountains around Dutch Harbor.
PHOTO VIA M.O.A. BLOOM COLLECTION

Detail of a painting commissioned by the National Guard showing their men firing a 3–inch AA gun during the attack on Dutch Harbor. Only one plane was shot down by AA fire.
GRAPHIC VIA ALASKA NATIONAL GUARD

THE ATTACKS ON DUTCH HARBOR

On June 3, 1942 a small flight of Japanese airplanes bombed the military installations at Dutch Harbor. These were the opening shots in the yearlong Aleutian campaign. The Japanese returned the next afternoon, dropping more bombs, killing more men, with much more accuracy than the previous morning. In the big picture damage was slight and casualties minimal, but for the men involved, especially the aviators, it was a frenzied, fearful experience.

> 25 May 1942
> From: CINCPAC (Commander in Chief, Pacific)
> To: COMNORPACFOR (Commander North Pacific Forces)
>
> THE JAPANESE HAVE COMPLETED PLANS FOR AN AMPHIBIOUS OPERA-TION TO SECURE AN ADVANCED BASE IN THE ALEUTIAN ISLANDS......FOLLOWING ESTIMATED JAPANESE TASK FORCE HAS LEFT JAPAN WITH PROBABLE OBJECTIVE ALEUTIAN ISLANDS AND/OR ALASKA: AIRCRAFT CARRIERS, 2-3 SEAPLANE TENDERS, 3 HEAVY CRUISERS, 2 LIGHT CRUISERS, 12 DESTROYERS, 8 SUBMARINES, HEAVY BOMBERS (PROBABLY FLYING BOATS) AND TRANSPORTS AND CARGO VESSELS...

At the twin bases of Ft. Mears and Naval Operating Base (NOB) Dutch Harbor, the men were aware of the potential attack. American code–breakers had let the Alaska Command know that the Japanese were planning to strike some time in late May or early June. Responding to this information, the entire post was put on alert each morning and evening, when the threat of attack was greatest. The men would head to the hills or their battle stations. After the half–hour alert normal duties were resumed.

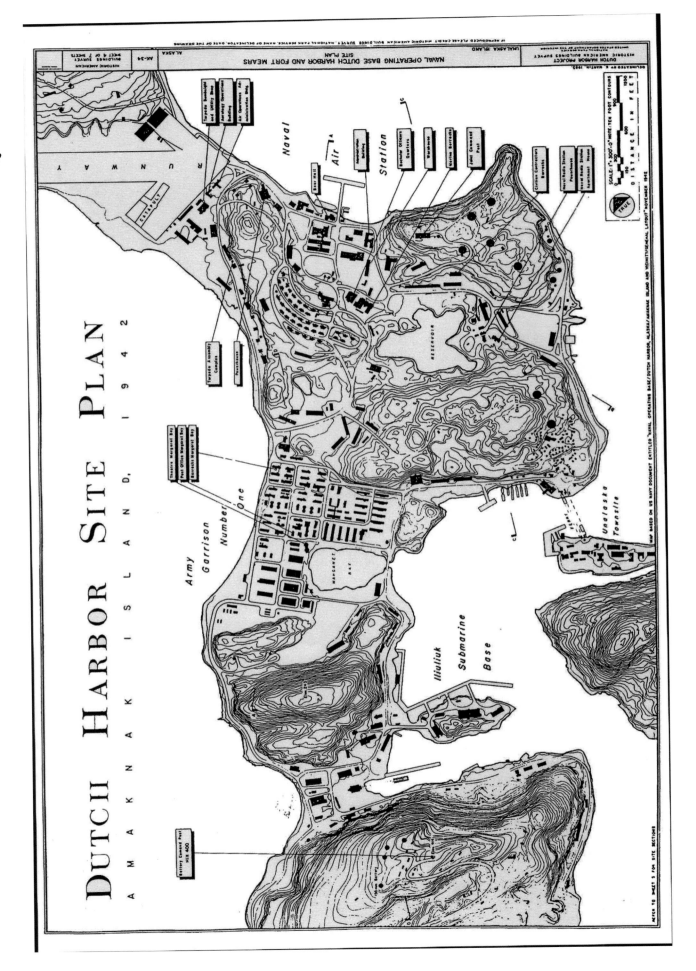

32

Marines defending Dutch Harbor man their trenches during a morning alert.

In order to spread out their forces, PBYs were dispersed to remote sites. Here three planes sit on the edge of Nikolski Lake, 100 miles west of Dutch.

In addition to the alerts, the patrol aircraft were dispersed each night. Planes would only be in Dutch Harbor to fuel up in the early morning or evening. They would spend their down time in a nearby bay. This was an effort to avoid the disaster of Pearl Harbor, at which nearly all of the U.S. planes were destroyed on the ground.

On June 3rd, the Japanese planes began their attack at 5:45AM. This was just after the morning alert had ended when many men headed for chow or morning showers. Some men had become inured to the daily alerts and slept in. It seemed another normal day until explosions let everyone know the attack was real.

THE JAPANESE OPERATION 3 JUNE

The Japanese sent two aircraft carriers with accompanying ships north to within 189 miles of Unalaska. They had not been observed despite PatWing–4's patrolling. They traveled within a storm front, hidden from American eyes. The day before the attack, a Japanese submarine had taken up station outside Unalaska Bay and reported good weather. When the Japanese planes launched from the carriers, however, half had to turn back due to low clouds and fog. The 21 planes that did fly on had no idea what the layout of the base was. Their primary target was to be the airfield followed by any radio facilities.

Left, a Japanese "Kate" bomber. It could carry five bombs or a torpedo. (File photo)

Below, the Japanese Zero. The fastest plane in the Pacific. (File Photo)

There were two types of planes, which arrived overhead that morning. Flying high and level were 13 Kate single–engine bombers. Really a torpedo plane, each bomber now carried one 550–lb. and four 150–lb. bombs. Flying low and fast, faster than any other plane in the Pacific, were the Zeros (sometimes called Zekes). Their mission was to protect the bombers and machine gun ground targets; they carried no bombs.

Finding no airfield, the Japanese pilots concentrated on radio antennas and other targets of opportunity. They were picked up on the radar of the seaplane tender U.S.S. *Gillis* tied up on the Ballyhoo Dock. The alarm was sounded across the base.

THE BOMBING OF DUTCH HARBOR 3 JUNE 1942

Don Sanders VP-41

We had morning and evening alerts, that is, from about a half–hour before daylight to a half–hour after and the same alert in the evenings. I wouldn't say we went to General Quarters, as our work station was really our GQ station.

The morning of the first raid, I was standing down from our "alert." I was among those who went to the barracks to eat and shower. When the first explosions occurred, I was in the shower. Whether from the building shaking from explosions or being startled, I fell. No doubt I slipped and/or went down more than once in my haste to get out of the shower. I neither rinsed nor toweled off before dressing.

Someone who outranked an AOM 2/c ordered a few of us into the "crawl" space beneath the barracks. Actually, there was about five feet of head space. I cannot speak for those with me, however, being under a building was not my idea of a place to be during an air raid.

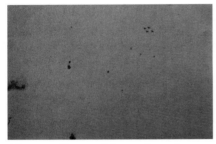

Above, a diamond formation of Kates flies high above Dutch Harbor, June 3rd.

Right, men hunker in their holes as Zeros fly low to strafe.

Ralph Erskine VP-41 (Journal entry)

3 June 1942. We got up at 0400, but nothing was happening, so we went back to our quarters and laid down. But not for long as the bombing and strafing began at 0545. The only ammunition we had to shoot were tracer bullets that had a fluorescent glow to them. Normally you fire one tracer bullet for every five regular bullets, so I guess the Japanese thought we were throwing up a lot of lead.

The Navy Base at Dutch Harbor. Beached inside the T dock is the S.S. *Northwestern*. It was used as a barracks, mess hall and power plant. The long parallel buildings are the navy barracks. The small houses were built for families but used by officers after the war broke out. The N.A.S. is off to the right a few hundred yards.

I spent the day at the Command Center erecting a portable transmitter with antennas and power supply. The men who stayed on their duty stations to work on planes only had jam sandwiches to eat, and we were only allowed one sandwich a day until the cooks got organized. They found some rice, and after that we had rice three times a day until more provisions arrived.

Bob Larson VP-41

Our crew was billeted in a frame house in Dutch Harbor known as the "aerology hut," because weather personnel were originally in it. A 37mm AA gun was located right next to the house. On June 3rd I was sleeping in my bed when the 37mm started shooting. Boy, was it loud! That was the first warning that an air raid was taking place. I pulled on my flight suit and jacket and headed for some kind of shelter. I jumped into a concrete stairwell that appeared to offer some shelter. I could see a formation of Kate bombers on their final run, but they were not directly overhead. I could see their bombs release, but I could estimate their trajectory, so I knew that I was relatively safe.

After the raid was over, I climbed up out of the stairwell and found that I had selected a spot right next to an ammunition cargo ship that was still full of high explosives. Had the Japanese put a bomb on that one, it would have blown up a considerably large area.

Bob Biddle VP-42

We made the pier at Dutch Harbor around 11PM the night before the attack. We were taken to the two-story barracks located close to the fuel oil tank farm. At 0500 we were awakened and sent to our air raid shelter underneath the barracks. Nothing happened so back topside to await breakfast. That was a meal I missed as the Jap planes began their attack. We got back

AA gun emplacements on a hilltop at Dutch Harbor.

into the "bomb shelter" and waited until things got a bit quiet. I knew I had to get to our planes that were parked in the revetments at the foot of Ballyhoo.

At the ripe old age of 17, I thought I was indestructible, so I took off running. Not far from the barracks on a high point I came upon a machine gun emplacement. As I recall, there were three or four bodies laying about, hit by strafing fire in all probability. I continued on and found my planes.

As an Aviation Ordinanceman, I was kept busy cleaning guns and hanging bombs. Our planes were coming and going every two or three hours, so sleep was hard to come by. I moved up on Ballyhoo and settled in with some Navy Seabees who fed me and woke me when a plane would arrive.

Vern Monckton VP-41

By the time we realized that we were being bombed, it was too late to do anything about it. It did appear that someone on our side seemed to be defending us, but I had no idea who it was. I found out later that it was soldiers. However, I was unaware that we shared the island with the Army that first day.

During one air raid alarm, another sailor and I were trying to stay out of harm's way when

A 37mm–gun crew readies more ammunition while others watch the oil tanks burn. Note WWI helmets and rifle.

A .50 cal. crew scans the skies for enemy aircraft. Mt. Ballyhoo towers above the base.

we discovered we had gone to school together. I don't recall which squadron he belonged to, there were people from VP-41 and VP-42 there at the time. I don't remember how it happened, but I became part of an Army group assigned to repel an invasion from the beach. I was assigned a foxhole and given a BAR (Browning Automatic Rifle) with ammunition and rifle grenades. I have no idea what I would have done if the attack had really come.

Frank Browning VP-41

On the first attack on June 3, Dutch Schultz, one of our senior Chiefs, manned the 50–cal. machine gun on the seaplane apron. When a Zero came in low from the north, strafing the area, he hunkered down in the sandbagged revetment. As the plane passed over, he stood up and "shot him in the ass." It was a no–deflection shot at close range, and he said the plane was smoking pretty good as it cleared the low hills to the south.

THE NAVAL AIR STATION

A PBY was in the process of taking off on the morning mail run to Kodiak. It was spotted by strafing Zeros and shot up on the water. The pilot, Lt. Jack Litsey, managed to beach the dam-

The N.A.S. hanger as it appeared during the attacks. The walls were not yet added. After the bombing it was removed to make room for a runway.

37

aged plane on the mile–long spit, which creates the harbor. It did not explode or burn and was salvaged. Two men were killed by bullets. A third, when wounded, jumped out the rear of the plane and drowned trying to reach shore less than 30 feet away.

Bill Thies VP-41

Whether I have dreamed it or whether it was true, I think I was at Dutch during the first raid and was probably in a foxhole. It seems to me, I remember seeing Jack Litsey crash on the spit after a Zero shot him up, but I am not sure. When you are scared sh...less, I guess the memory faculties just don't function.

Ed Froehlich VP-41

We were scheduled for patrol at 1100 June 3rd. The attack by the Jap Zeros started around 0600, shooting up Lt.(Jg) Litsey on the take off, killing three men, he ditched and abandoned his PBY on the spit. They also attacked Jim Hildebrand who was airborne, his crew shot up the Zero, and he got away flying up a gully out of Dutch.

Carl Hagaman VP-41

The Japs started their approach, and all hell broke loose. I jumped up, looked out the second floor door nearest the hanger as a Jap plane was making a run at an antiaircraft gun on the point between me and the hanger. His bomb fell short and exploded near a man making his way to the ramp. Needless to say he disappeared and that afternoon I had to lead the medics to pick up his body.

Ralph Morrison VP-42

On June 3, 1942 Ens. Ortman and myself were assigned as passengers aboard a PBY-5A flown by LT. (Jg) Litsey and Ens. Syd Eland. Ens. Ortman and myself had been erroneously dropped at Dutch Harbor by the ship that brought us from Seattle. Lt. Litsey was to drop us at Cold Bay to join VP-42. Ens. Ortman positioned himself in the main cabin. I chose to stay in the blister area.

On the takeoff run in the bay I heard a crackling noise, which I assumed to be a short in the electrical system. To back up my theory, a tracer hit the fire extinguisher mounted just ahead of me. In my innocence, I assumed it to be St. Elmo's Fire.

The fighter(s) that attacked us was a pretty good shot. I later counted about 100 holes in the hull alone. In the process he (they) knocked out one engine while we were still on the water. On the one remaining engine Lt. Litsey was attempting to head for the spit in the harbor.

Subsequently the order was given to abandon ship. With all my heavy flight gear (fleece–lined boots. fleece–lined pants, fleece–lined jacket), I didn't hanker to go swimming if I could help it, so I stayed long enough to take off my boots. While I was removing the boots two crew went over the side.

When I hit the water I tried to find the pull cords on my life jacket which, unfortunately, was under my flight jacket. I couldn't find them. Now I was in dire straits. I figured I would sink like a rock as soon as my clothes got water–soaked. When I looked up the two crew who had gone over the side ahead of me were wading in water not over three feet deep.

Ens. Ortman had his hand on the radioman's back during the takeoff run. A bullet pierced his hand, passed through the radioman's heart and landed, spent, on the radioman's type-writer keys.

Sometime during the day (June 3) the airplane was moved to a corner of the partially com-pleted hanger. Contrary to every book written on the subject, the aircraft did not burn. In the

Lt. Litsey's PBY lies on the beach were it drifted after being shot up and rammed ashore on the spit. A bomb destroyed it the next day.
PHOTO VIA H. KNIGHT

second attack (June 4) a bomb was dropped behind the plane and did a good job of accordion-pleating it.

H. "Hoot" Smith VP-42

I felt the concussion of the bomb and the barracks was sprinkled with shrapnel. Later, I was able to obtain several pieces as souvenirs. It wasn't long until I made my way to the stairs and down to the shelter under the barracks.

In due time, "All Clear" sounded, and we proceeded to the ramp. Lt. Litsey's plane was brought up the ramp and pushed in the hanger. We went to work on it, and most of the holes were repaired temporarily so it could be salvaged.

FT. MEARS

The first wave of four Kate bombers dropped a string of 16 bombs on Ft. Mears. The first two bombs fell into water. The next two hit barracks 864 and 866. A ship load of new troops had off-loaded the night before and were not told to take shelter at 0430. In the confusion an officer of the 151st Combat Engineers ordered his men to fall into ranks. Eight of his men and 17 men from the 37th Infantry were killed. Twenty-five men were wounded. The rest of the bombs fell in a line, destroying three warehouses, three Quonsets and two cold storage buildings. Several vehicles in the area were also damaged. In one of the warehouses was a valuable radar set, destroyed in the attack.

HILL NORTH END OF FT. MEARS

Three Kates attacked from the north. A string of six bombs fell in a line across a small hill just outside the buildings of Ft. Mears. They killed one soldier and blew out some windows in a barracks (building #644)

NAVAL RADIO STATION

Another flight of three Kates dropped the third string of bombs. The target was the Naval Radio Station located behind the Red Brick Building, marked by tall antennas. The first

Right, the tightly packed buildings of Ft. Mears. Lack of flat ground forced the base to build close together. The white paint was standard for all U.S. garrisons. It was in the process of being changed in June.

Below, a destroyed Mess Hall, Ft. Mears.
PHOTO VIA M.O.A. POWELL COLLECTION

Right, destroyed barracks, Ft. Mears. Twenty–five men were killed in this string of bombs.
PHOTO VIA M.O.A. POWELL COLLECTION

Below, in addition to bombs, the Zeros strafed the base with machine gun fire.

Right, white xs mark the string of bombs, which covered this hill on the north edge of Ft. Mears.

Below, the back of this building was showered with shrapnel.

41

The barracks and two warehouses
caught fire and burned dramatically.

bomb narrowly missed the building, shattering some windows. The sixth bomb destroyed a Quonset hut and the fifth buried a civilian construction worker, killing him. The others did no damage.

Ed Froehlich VP-41

42

VP-41 Chief Petty Officers were housed in the Radio Tower, (red brick building) where I was at that time, the Japs strafed us and high altitude bombed us, near misses, but none of the VP-41 CPOs were injured. One Seims–Drake employee was killed in a Quonset nearby.

POWER HOUSE HILL

At least five bombs fell on and around Power House Hill. Their target was either a radio antenna or nearby fuel tanks. One bomb buried a Marine private killing him. Another landed in

After the white, tightly packed Ft. Mears, this antenna farm was the next target.

The red brick building and antennas were completely obscured by the bomb blasts.

The building, housing C.P.O.s was not hit, but all the windows were blown out.

Ironically, a Quonset hut designated as a bomb shelter for civilian construction workers was totally destroyed.

At the time of the attacks hundreds of civilians were employed as construction workers. They were soon shipped out and replaced by Navy Seabees. BLOOM COLLECTION M.O.A.

the middle of Biorka Road, about 100 yards from the beach, killing a truck driver, a nearby sailor and wounding a third. Three bombs hit soft ground and did no damage.

Jack Kassel VP-42

I had just returned from a patrol mission and was pulling off my flight boots, when the first stick of bombs straddled across the civilian construction houses, at the top of the hill, where we flyers lived. I dove through the side door and jumped into the trash pit between the houses. Anyplace to dodge the bombs!

Ralph Erskine VP-41

After the attack some of the NAS sailors panicked, because they believed that they were going to be taken by the Japanese so they opened food lockers and took food with them up to the foxholes on Mount Ballyhoo. They left the frozen food lockers open and all of the food that was left spoiled.

At the end of the Officer's housing sat a small radio shack, surrounded by tall antennas. This was the next target.

"That one knocked me off my feet!" was the message supposedly sent out by the radio operator as bombs surrounded the shack.

Officers climb in the bomb crater 100 yards from the radio shack.

A view of the explosions from Mt. Ballyhoo.

Above, small concrete bomb shelters were interspersed around the base. This one was filled, overflowing with men when the bomb hit 50 feet away.

Left, the same bomb killed the driver of this truck. The man in the foreground stands in the crater.

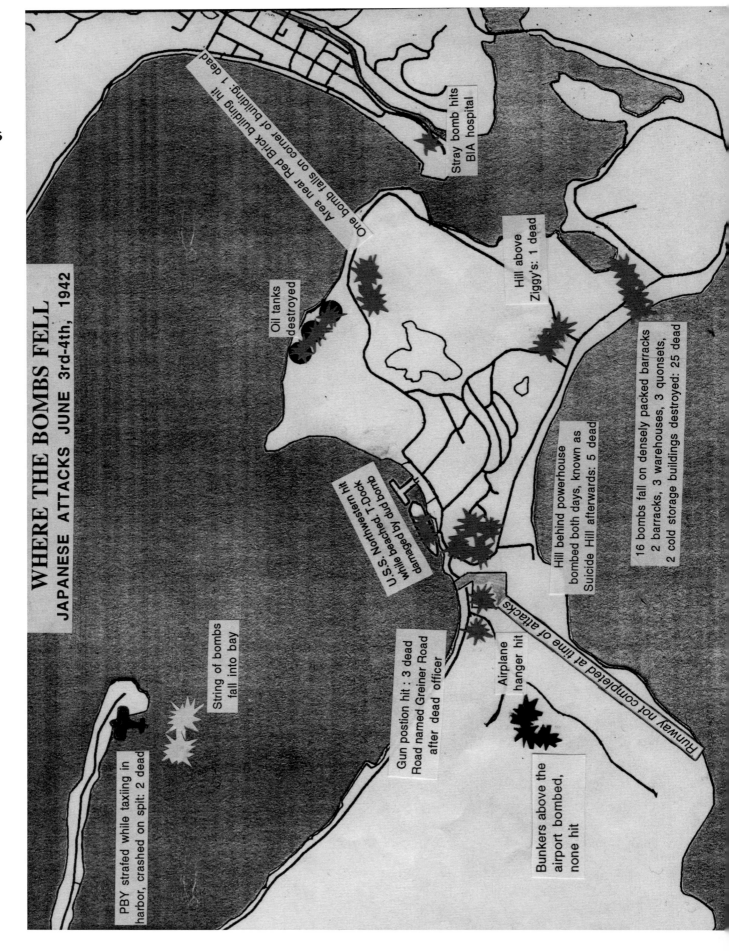

WHERE THE BOMBS FELL
JAPANESE ATTACKS JUNE 3rd-4th, 1942

Area near Red Brick building hit
One bomb falls on corner of building : 1 dead

Stray bomb hits
BIA hospital

Hill above
Ziggy's : 1 dead

Oil tanks
destroyed

16 bombs fall on densely packed barracks
2 barracks, 3 warehouses, 3 quonsets,
2 cold storage buildings destroyed: 25 dead

Hill behind powerhouse
bombed both days, known as
Suicide Hill afterwards: 5 dead

U.S.S. Northwestern hit
while beached by T-Dock
damaged by dud bomb

String of bombs
fall into bay

Gun postion hit : 3 dead
Road named Greiner Road
after dead officer

Airplane
hanger hit

Runway not completed at time of attacks

PBY strafed while taxiing in
harbor, crashed on spit: 2 dead

Bunkers above the
airport bombed,
none hit

THE EXPERIENCES OF PATROL WING FOUR IN THE AIR JUNE 2-5, 1942

When the word came that the Japanese were headed for the Aleutians, the men and machines of PatWing–4 went into high gear. Patrols were launched in every direction, including north over the Bering Sea. On June 3, PPC Bill Thies' log shows he and his crew flew to Umnak, loaded bombs and a torpedo and took off for an 11–hour patrol. This was what every plane in the wing was doing—looking for the Japanese fleet. Their job was to locate the Japanese fleet and radio its position back to the Army bases where B-26 bombers were waiting, loaded with torpedoes. Army airplane crews had little training in navigating over trackless ocean, so it was decided to keep them on the ground to wait for the patrol plane reports.

Since the PBYs were Navy planes, they were originally based out of Dutch Harbor. In order to extend the coverage area, VP-42 was based out of the Army base in Cold Bay. The VP-41 PBYs flying out of Dutch had no landing strip. Operating off from the water limited their takeoff weight, so with a minimal load they would fly west 45 minutes to the Army base on Umnak.

Bill Thies VP-41

Taking off from Dutch and topping off at Umnak—if I remember correctly, when we did that, it was for two reasons. One, we had to go to Umnak to load torpedoes, when that was the mission, and topped off while we were there. Dutch, to the best of my memory, didn't store torpedoes. Two, if it was going to be on an extended search to the very limits of our capability,

48

Three B-26s awaiting orders, Cold
Bay airfield.

in a sector south and/or south and west of Umnak, we could get a another hour or two by taking on gas at Umnak. There was a small contingent in Umnak, like the Chief Torpedoman, a few mechs for minor repairs and fueling, communications, etc. We got all our food from Dutch.

Patrols lasted 10-12 hours. Each plane was assigned a pie–shaped sector, usually 600 miles out, 100 miles across and back. Since the planes had radar, searches continued at night. When the Japanese fleet was within striking distance, the patrol planes were putting out a maximum effort to locate the fleet and stay out of harm's way.

Bill Thies VP-41

During the time of the Japanese attack up there, we normally went on patrol every other day or every third day depending on number of planes and crews available. There were a couple of occasions when we came in, gassed up and went right back out.

Bob Larson VP-41

We were flying almost continuously except for occasional rest periods. Perhaps I mentioned this before, but we did three consecutive patrols in a 48–hour period. I have never been so tired. I really don't know how Bill Thies stayed awake. Actually he didn't. One time I fell asleep at the navigation table. When I awoke I couldn't find a single crewman awake. It's a good thing the autopilot was working well.

Vern Monckton VP-41

Life then entered an uneasy period at Dutch Harbor for there were constant rumors when we were not sure what the Japanese were going to do. The flight crews were constantly in the air, working on their planes, or exhausted in their bunks. The ground crews were busy trying to keep as many planes in flying condition as possible. As an indication of the exhausted state of the flight crews: one of the Patrol Plane Commanders (PPCs) had his hat on backwards as he was going up the hill to the command post when he met the Commander coming down the hill. The Commander reminded him that he wasn't in uniform. The PPC replied, "Hell, Commander I am so tired I don't know if am coming or going," and kept on up the hill.

Above, a group of PatWing–4 pilots walking towards the N.A.S. Dutch Harbor, June 4.

Left, it was not uncommon to catch a few winks while on endless patrol over the North Pacific.
PHOTO VIA H. FORT

A PBY was built to be the eyes of the Navy, not the fist. Its bomb load was small, its defenses woefully weak. Its job was to locate the enemy fleet and then shadow it well out of range and hopefully out of sight. All aircraft carriers and airfields had a combat air patrol (CAP)—a small group of fighters fly high over the carrier ready to pounce on any threat. A Japanese Zero fighter would make short work of a PBY. The American P-boat pilots would fly in and out of the clouds, trying hard to see but not be seen.

When the enemy was located the patrol plane would stay on station until their fuel ran low. Often the PPC would make a bomb or torpedo run on the ships. The PBY was not built for offensive action, and most who tried this were either shot down or damaged. The planes slow speed and the need to fly straight and level to drop bombs made it an easy target for enemy anti-aircraft guns and planes.

The adventures of the PBY men started before the enemy fleet was located. The Americans knew the Japanese fleet was out there and were pushing their machines to the limit looking for it.

Ed Froehlich VP-41

Returning from patrol on 1 June '42 we could not get into Dutch Harbor due to impossible weather. "Wait an hour," the base advised us by code message. We didn't have enough fuel left for an hour, so Mr. Bowers decided to go back through the pass past Egg Island and land on the lee side of Unalaska. The wind was about 60 mph out of the Northwest and visibility less than a quarter mile at 50 feet altitude. Sissenwood guiding us by radar, which was very new then. Anyway we wound up in a dead end channel on the west side of Beaver Inlet, after a lot of gray hair. Mr. Bowers advised us that our best bet was sail the plane across Beaver Inlet into a channel on the east side where three buoys had been anchored for this very purpose. The water was too deep on the west side to anchor 50 feet from the shore, which was a mountain straight up into the overcasts.

The channel we got to after the rough trip across the Inlet had no buoys—probably the wrong channel. The low engine (the port) died en route, no gas. The starboard (high engine) was running ok, but turning with one engine in the high wind and rough waters was impossible. We could see the waves hitting the rocks at the end of the channel, spray going 50 feet high. Mr. Bowers told me to get the rubber rafts ready, and we would abandon the PBY before hitting the rocks. Suddenly, as we drifted by a point of rocks, a sandy beach about 200 feet long and maybe 30 feet wide before the mountain went up into the overcast, a beach showed up on the port side. Mr. Bowers used the Starboard engine to turn the plane onto this beach. We man-handled the PBY-5A in waist deep water around so the wheels were against the beach, secured the tail and wing tips to the anchor and some bushes. We survived the violent williwaws all night wet, cold and hungry, rough night.

The next day (2 June 42) a YP boat from Dutch Harbor brought us fuel and food, about mid-afternoon we loaded the anchor, cut the line to the bushes and taxied down through the rocks into the water and flew back to Dutch Harbor. We were scheduled for patrol at 1100 the next day, 3 June. The attack by the Jap Zeros started around 0600.

Paul Cleveland VP-41

On 2 June 1942 our flight crew in 41-P-5 upon return from a 10-hour patrol to Dutch Harbor, received word over the radio of the Japanese attack and dispersed to Umnak field and then later in the day flew back to Dutch Harbor.

First blood was drawn before the Japanese planes had reached Dutch Harbor. A flight of Zeros and Vals had taken off the morning of the 3rd. Within an hour they had been turned back because of the weather. On their way back they encountered 41-P-5, a PBY flow by PPC Cusick and crewed by eight others.

Carl Creamer VP-41

On June 2, several of us in PBY-5As flew to Umnak to help unload bombs and torpedoes on the steel mat. Next morning, we left at 0300 for our return flight to Dutch Harbor. At daybreak we ran into a group of Japanese bombers and fighters coming into Dutch. We went into a cloud bank, and when we came out there were three to four Zeros waiting for us. Before we could get back into the clouds, a Zero lined up on our tail and shot completely through our plane. I was standing on the cat walk just behind our pilot, Lt. Jean Cusick, facing starboard, drinking a cup of coffee. The coffee was knocked out of my hand when bullets hit my right sleeve and pant legs. I am sure that the same bullets hit Lt. Cusick on the portside and 1st class AP (our second pilot) Morrison on the starboard. I also think that both Cusick and Morrison were crushed by the pilots yoke when we crashed because neither fellow lived long after we got out of the aircraft. We were finally picked up by a Japanese cruiser after being in the water about four hours. Wylie Hunt, Joe Brown and I were the only survivors from the nine men on the PBY.

51

The Japanese may have left them, but after the bombing of Dutch, their planes had been jumped by American fighters over Umnak. The Japanese wanted to know where those planes had come from. Hunt, the only officer, was taken to the rail of the ship, bound, blindfolded with a weight tied around his waist. At the end of a bayonet he was questioned about the American fighters. He feigned ignorance hoping his crewmates would as well. They did and the Japanese, convinced he knew nothing, returned him below. All three survived three and a half years as prisoners in Japan.

The Japanese scored their second victory within minutes of arriving over Dutch Harbor.

Frank Browning VP-41

On June 3, Litsey was scheduled for the mail run to Kodiak. This was the closest thing we had to offer for R&R, and we rotated the assignment among the pilots. Jack was scheduled to take off at 0530 and should have been clear of the area before the attack came in. But he overslept and was still on the water on his takeoff run at 0600 when he got shot up by a Zero. He beached the plane on the spit, and we later recovered it and put it in the hangar for repair. The plane had many bullet holes but no major structural damage, but the following afternoon the Japs returned. One bomb went through the hanger roof and really ruined that PBY. It then became the "Hanger Queen" and a valuable source of parts.

Inside Litsey's plane two men were killed and a couple wounded. Litsey beached the damaged machine 0n the beach, and one of the wounded men climbed out the rear blister window and drowned trying to reach the shore less that 30 feet away. The plane did not burn or explode.

The following is an attempt to account for all of PatWing–4's PBYs during June 3 and 4. Planes are identified by PPC name or plane number. Many short entries are from the VP-42 war diary,the others from veteran's accounts.

Coming into Dutch from an all night patrol, Lt. Dickey's radioman called with an "In" report. He was told to land at a dispersal point and await further orders. Around noon they were given permission to fly to Dutch. From there they were ordered to do a 12–hour daylight search north, over the Bering Sea.

Thirty miles to the east, dispersed in Akutan Bay, three PBYs (Hildebrand, Boyle, Campbell) got the word via radio that Dutch was being attacked. They set up their machine guns on shore in case the Japanese found them. At 0730 they were ordered from Dutch to patrol south of the chain. They took off at 0830.

Radioman John Mumma's plane was returning to Dutch after a night patrol out west. They landed in Chernofski Harbor on the west end of Unalaska when they heard Dutch was under attack. They anchored the PBY and paddled the plane's rubber boats to shore, waiting until they got the all clear from the base.

Lt. Boyle, VP-41, on patrolling south from Akutan, encountered two enemy float biplanes, which fired at him. Without locating the carriers, he landed at Cold Bay at 12:30, refueled and flew back to Dutch.

Ens. Hildebrand, VP-41, encountered two Japanese carrier planes southwest of Unalaska and exchanged shots with them.

Lt. Campbell's PBY patrolled parallel to Unalaska, 100 miles south. Soon, they saw an enemy scout plane. At 1140 they picked up two planes on radar. Twenty minutes later they picked up four or five ships via radar. George Thelen VP-42, was the navigator on the plane:

George Thelen VP-42

I arrived here (Dutch Harbor) on the 29th of May 1942, and I made my first flight on June 1st as part of the crew. I remember that was a long flight. We ended up somewhere on some other island in a little cove and waited until the fog lifted the next morning to get in to Dutch. The next day, the 3rd—the big day—we picked up a plane that had come back from a night flight, and we got up at 4AM and picked up that airplane and flew over to Akutan. That was to be our dispersal for the day, we would rest there, then later, we would take off and go over to Umnak and load fuel and armament if we needed it. The plane still had the bombs on it and the torpedo. Then take our flight looking for the fleet. As we touched down at Akutan, we got the word by radio, Morse code, "Dutch was under attack." We had just left there. We knew the plane was short on fuel from flying all night, so we thought, "Well, we better get ready what fuel we can into this thing."

They had fuel barrels there at the old whaling station, and they had a boat. We got three barrels and a hand pump into the boat and brought it out to the airplane. We got 150 gallons into the plane and got the word to take off immediately and search for the fleet. We only had 300 gallons of fuel in the airplane, not very much. We headed south, staying low because of clouds. We fly out there, and we hadn't seen anything. About noon we decided to turn back before we lost it. Somewhere, shortly after that, as we headed back, all of a sudden we hear these bullets coming in through the hull of the airplane and ricocheting around and some were tracers and all this racket.

George Thelen drew this sketch of his PBY getting attacked by a Zero over Unimak Pass.

A fighter had come up behind us. He was either coming to Dutch or returning to the carrier. He saw us and fired upon us. The two rear gunners didn't see him. One was hit in the leg. At the same time he shot one of the two struts away on the right wing. Fortunately, it angled up and didn't hit the prop. If he had, we would have had it, because he also shot our rudder controls away. With only one engine and ailerons you're not gonna control a big old airplane like that. We had ailerons and two engines still running, so we pulled up in the stuff to lose him. We also happened to see a break in the clouds, and here was the fleet and it wasn't ours. But we didn't have time to send much more than "We have sighted the fleet" in Morse code, but the message was garbled—they don't know why.

In the meantime, we continued to evade. Our radar showed objects approaching, probably fighters coming back, so we kept doing this and that, and I was navigating to track us. We broke out one time, and we saw the tip of Shishalden Volcano, which meant we were quite a ways east of Dutch. We figured we'd better get down into the clouds again and about that time both engines quit. Dead stick...down through about 8,000 feet of clouds and fog. We broke out below the clouds at about 300 feet. The PPC and copilot pulled back on the yoke to flare the thing. As they did, some fuel was left in a sump, which fed one engine. So it went to full power on one side with no rudder, and we were getting close to the waves. They were able to man-handle it back just in time to straighten it out and hit. This was about 3:00 in the afternoon. The airplane was leaking from bullet holes, so we started bailing and plugging up the holes. We also got the two life rafts out in case we needed them. We pretty well controlled the sinking part of it. We were pretty dry, semi-dry in there.

Another of Thelen's drawings showing their rescue.

Later, about an hour, another PBY came by. He was lost. He saw us on the water, flew over and signaled as to what the location was. We figured where we were and signaled back to them. He took that information and set his course back to Dutch. On the way he ran across a Coast Guard Cutter, the Nemaha. He flew over the deck and dropped a message in a sack with a wrench in it. It gave our position and that we needed help. The Nemaha was headed in that direction. His orders were to leave the area if hostilities broke out. He was headed for Kodiak.

Right as it was getting dusk—11:30PM—we see a searchlight on the horizon. OK, Japanese? We were in pretty poor shape, so we took a chance and signaled back. It was very fortunate, as the Captain had turned the ship and one of the sailors saw our light behind them. We used the life rafts to get to his rescue boat and transferred the crew to the U.S.C.C. Nemaha. We tried to tow the airplane, but the seas were so rough it kept nosing under, so we finally sank it with machinegun fire.

We headed on then, under radio silence, to the Shumagins then to Kodiak where the Wing Commander wanted a full report. Then we were flown back to Cold Bay, where the headquarters of the squadron was. This was the first they knew that we were alive. We had quite a reception.
(from and interview by Ray Hudson and Jeff Dickrell on the 50th anniversary of the event)

Campbell and crew were the only Americans to contact the Japanese fleet that day. Thelen recorded the weather as: ceiling 400-800 ft rain above that 2,000-3,000 ft above that snow and severe icing. They searched using radar just below the icing layer.

A Coast Guard cutter on patrol in the Aleutians.

Ens. Kirmse was PPC of the PBY that found Thelen's plane. Kirmse was also reported to have flown into a dogfight over Umnak later that day.

Lt.(jg) Stockstill VP-42 was in Kodiak, quickly flew to Cold Bay and was ordered to patrol 200 miles south of Sand Point.

Ens. Doerr VP-41 encountered the Japanese attackers after the bombing raid on Dutch. Bob Spence was on that plane:

Bob Spence VP-41

The plane captain was a Chief (Petty Officer), which was unusual, and he spotted the Japanese first that day. We came out of the clouds and Sandy yelled "Japs." He didn't say where, and we're all frantically looking around. It turned out we were going this way, and they were down on the port side, ahead of us coming towards us. But they were quite a ways down. There were four Zeros and four bombers, and they were coming back from bombing Dutch.

We were on our way to Umnak that morning...we were the last plane off ahead of Litsey. Our unit got us (on the radio) right after we got out there and told us what was happening and told us to go look for the carriers. So we went out way short of fuel, and because of that we were coming back in the middle of the day. We were just about out of fuel, we were coming in, and the Japanese had bombed and were coming back to their carrier. The lead Zero then peeled off, and he pulled his airplane into what is called a pursuit curve with which they catch up with you and strafe your airplane end to end. He was coming around and up, and I was firing a 50–cal. from the waist of the port side right down in his face, and he broke off and slide under the airplane. In the meantime Doerr and Carpenter had yanked the nose of the PBY up hard, because we had just come out of the clouds, and they were still close and we went popping up into the clouds and both engines stopped cold. They mashed the nose down—we were pretty weightless in the back. By this time we were in the clouds and they got the nose down and the engines started running again and we were alive. It had run out of gas due to the gravity fuel system. That was a tense moment.

We stayed up in the clouds for awhile, but we still had to go home because we were rapidly running out of fuel. We went into Dutch Harbor. By that time, we knew by radio that they were OK. We had about 20 holes in the airplane, but we only had a couple of bad rips in the fabric of the control surfaces. One bullet had come in about four inches from my left knee, and that was as far forward as any bullets got. We had a brand new radioman. His name was Junior Reed. He was in back scrambling around (because it was his first flight) trying to get this stupid tunnel gun, which was a peashooter if you ever saw one, but he was trying to get the thing out, and a lot of bullets came around him. It never touched him, and when it was all over I looked around—Junior was as white as a tablecloth, and you could stand and count his freckles. I had figured that he was gone because I knew we had taken some hits back there. No one in the plane was hit. Even though the airplane was in pretty fair shape, they didn't want to let it fly that way, so they had it in a revetment in Dutch where they were gonna fix it the next day.

At 0710 the morning of June 4th, a PBY piloted by Lt. Freerks finishing a night patrol, made visual contact with the Japanese. They had gotten a reading on their radar and followed it up. The ships were south of Adak preparing to launch an attack. Freerks performed his mission perfectly, reporting the location, weather and disposition of the enemy. Bad weather prevented the Japanese from launching a Combat Air Patrol (CAP). For the next hour he shadowed the fleet, flying in and out of clouds. Freerks had to leave the scene, low on fuel. He tried a bomb run but was shot up by anti–aircraft fire.

With Freerk's location reports a steady stream of patrol planes kept vigil. Soon a VP-42 plane (PPC Lt. Stockstill) arrived to take over the mission. Unfortunately, the Japanese had been able to launch their CAP. Stockstill and his crew were lost, recorded by the Japanese as shot down in flames. Robert Brown was a part of Stockstill's crew and perhaps the luckiest man in the Wing.

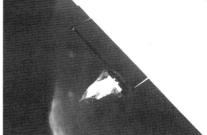

Bob Spence's crew examines their riddled PBY after running into Japanese Zeroes.

Robert Brown VP-42

Our plane had to go to Kodiak for a propeller replacement. Day, our Plane Capt., told Secord and me only one could go; the other would be dropped off at Sand Point (near Cold Bay). We matched and I lost. After dropping me off, I was given a gun and told to patrol the beach. They knew something was coming up.

Then on June 3rd they did stop by to pick me up. I was still patrolling the beach. They were ordered to shadow the Jap fleet that had been sighted. (They left without picking him up.) They were spotted and shot down in flames.

Not aware of this, some other sailors and I were put aboard the USS Williamson *for another base. Enroute we were attacked by some Zeros. No major damage to the ship. We were on deck, running from port to starboard on each strafing run. I remember one of the ship's personnel being shot in the eye.*

While avoiding the Zeros, one of us spotted a periscope quite some distance from our ship. My first thought was, "Not now! This ship is a plane tender, loaded with gas and bombs." A few

Above, this sailor was manning this position on the 5–inch AA gun on the USS *Williamson*. His eye was lost by a ricocheting bullet. The dent made by the bullet can be seen on the metal across from his face. Left, the official caption of this photo simply states, "PBY crew after action against Japanese."

Above, an aerial view of the cannery at Sand Point, Alaska. Located in the Shumagin Islands, south of Cold Bay airfield.
Right, Sand Point was used as a dispersal base for PatWing–4. Here a PBY taxis up to the cannery in spring of 1942.

minutes later an American flag unfolded from the periscope. Boy, what a beautiful sight. Don't know how they did it. I have been told it can't be done. But I know what I saw, regardless of what others say.

On arriving at our base I was informed our ship was searching for one of our planes, not knowing it was mine. The Chief Petty Officer was asking questions about Lt. Stockstill's crew when my name came up. Then I knew my plane had been shot up.

My future Plane Captain, Noel Hanson, was on the Williamson *with me as he had gotten some gas in his eyes when filling his plane. His plane was also shot down. One of the crew, Rawls, got out of the plane and into a life raft when the Jap shot and killed him. (This was Lt. Mitchell's PBY shot down near Unalaska Island.)*

The Japanese planes that shot up the *Williamson* were returning to the carriers. Their rendezvous point was Ship Rock located in the pass between Umnak and Unalaska. It was also just off shore of the Army's airbase. When the Japanese Kates, Vals and Zeros started circling around the rally point, American P-40s from the 11th fighter squadron, on Combat Air Patrol, swooped in and quickly shot down two Vals. P-40s from the ground got airborne. Two of the American fighters were shot down. One pilot survived the crash of his plane near the beach on Unalaska.

A P-40 at Umnak, May 1942. These were the first line of defense in the air above the Aleutians. They were not scrambled in time to interrupt the attacks.

Four P-40s buzz the field at Umnak.

The USS *Williamson*, tender for the Wing, caught by Japanese fighters near Umnak Pass.

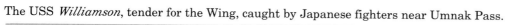

Above, Ens. Hilderbrand in the cockpit of his PBY. He and his crew were lost tracking the Japanese fleet.
PHOTO VIA PATWING 4 COLLECTION
Right, Robert Blair snapped this shot of a B-26 flying towards the Aleutians. Note the torpedo racks underneath the fuselage.
PHOTO VIA ROBERT BLAIR

Before plunging into the sea, Lt. John Cape shot down a Zero. (The field at Umnak was named in his honor.) Two more Vals were shot up so bad they never made it back to the carriers. One other Val became lost trying to find the Japanese ships and disappeared. Japanese losses for the two days of attacks were: two Zeros and five Vals. Only one Zero was shot down over Dutch. Every available PBY was diverted to the west. A VP-42 P-boat (PPC Perkins) arrived at 11:05AM to continue observations. Another plane piloted by Ens. Hildebrand of VP-41 also joined the airspace. Both planes circled the Japanese, evading the Zeros looking for them. Low on fuel, Perkins dropped down to make a torpedo run before heading for base. Launching a torpedo from a plane takes a low, slow steady approach close to the target, usually against an enemy who is fully alerted. In a large, slow PBY this is nearly suicide. He reported, "Attack not completed. Engine destroyed. returning to base." Dumping his torpedo, he turned his plane to the east and wrangled it back to Dutch Harbor, where he landed safely. "Hoot" Smith VP-42 was the navigator on Perkin's plane. This is his, somewhat deadpan, diary entry of that flight.

H. "Hoot" Smith VP-42

Thurs. June 4th 1942   Fog occasionally broken. Up at 3:30. Took off and searched Tigalda Is. for missing VP-41 plane. Talked to the USS Gillis *blinker. Got orders to attack Jap carriers, W, 240 miles. Sighted Jap task force of one carrier (it was two) 2 cruisers, several cans [tincans = destroyers] at about 11:00AM Flew over three times at 1500 ft, fourth time cruiser opened up with A.A. [antiaircraft fire] and hit our port engine [oil tank and gas line] full feathered prop. Dropped torpedo and two 500–lb. bombs. 250 gals to go and 110 miles from home. Several shells burst near the plane. In at 1500 Beached by crash boat.*

Hildebrand's plane simply disappeared. Japanese records make no mention of the plane. The crew was listed as an operational loss not a combat one.

Reacting to the location reports, five Army B-26s took off from Umnak. They never located the Japanese and returned to base. Five more B-26s took off from Cold Bay with the same mission. Three of these turned back, but two kept on, finding the enemy fleet. They were armed with torpedoes and attempted to attack. The twin–engine bomber piloted by Capt. Taylor was shot up by anti–aircraft fire and a CAP of Zeros and fled after three attempts at launching his torpedo. Capt. Thornborough tried twice to launch his torpedo, finally dropping it like a bomb. It narrowly missed a carrier. Both planes returned to Cold Bay. Thornborough rearmed with bombs but was lost trying to find the base after an unsuccessful search for the Japanese.

58

A PBY sits next to a B-26 at the ready at Cold Bay.

June 4th also found a couple PBYs (Thies and Breeding) loading torpedoes at Umnak. When they heard the location report and saw six torpedo–loaded B-26s ready to go they took action. The following statement was found in an Army Air Force report.

Lt. Breeding VP-41

Receiving orders to land at Umnak and load with torpedoes we found five or six B-26s loaded with torpedoes. There would be quite some delay in loading our torpedoes, due to equipment shortages. Bill Thies and I contacted Col. Foster to see if they would take off on attack. Col. Foster said he was taking orders from Lt. Cmdr. Foley, and he suggested to the pilots of the B-26s that they stay on the ground until orders were received. Due to the fact that the enemy forces were located and a PBY was sending MOs and tracking the enemy, we felt all planes available should be attacking. When I suggested to Col. Foster that I send a message to L/C Foley telling him of the B-26s awaiting his orders, the Col. told me not to do it and stay right where I was. I disregarded his orders and sent the following message, "Six B-26s loaded with torpedoes here awaiting your orders for takeoff. PBYs are loading torpedoes." Orders came immediately from Foley for the B-26s to take off immediately. During our conversation with Col. Foster, he repeatedly said that he was taking orders from the Navy, from someone 14 years his junior.

There was a good reason that the B-26s were not overly aggressive. Army pilots were never trained to use torpedoes, a Navy weapon. Plus, torpedoes were slung under the B-26s with six inches of clearance. This was not a comfort on the rough airfields of the Aleutians.

Robert Blair, B-26 pilot 77th Squadron

We had torpedo missions planned, but I never took off with one. One pilot [Thompson] took off with a torpedo, was unable to find a target to drop it on and returned to base and landed. The torpedo broke loose from the shackles and bounced end over end alongside the plane but did not hit it. From then on we were instructed to jettison the torpedo if no target was available. We were on alert with torpedoes but made sure we had a target before taking off.

After the PBY observers had left the area of the Japanese task force, Adm. Kakuta ordered the launch of the second attack group. They flew around the east end of the island, where they encountered a VP-42 PBY flown by Ens. Mitchell. He was flying into Unalaska to deliver dis-

Above, Capt. Mendenhall shows off the low clearance of the torpedo mounted on his B-26.
Right, a trio of army ordnancemen stand around a naval torpedo. This was a new weapon to the Air Force flyers.

patches from Kodiak. He had just made landfall off the southeastern tip of Unalaska, near Egg Island, when his plane was swallowed by the mass of planes on their way to bomb Dutch Harbor. A group of three Zero fighters quickly shot down the patrol plane. The Japanese pilots then proceeded to strafe the survivors, who were struggling to gain the life rafts. This was witnessed by an Army observation post located on Fisherman's Point three miles away. A body and a riddled raft were recovered by ship later that day.

Just before their carriers south of Umnak Island recovered the Japanese planes, two Air Force B-17s found and dropped their bombs on the enemy fleet, without scoring a hit. One B-17 was shot down by the carrier's Zeros. At 9PM, June 4, three B-26s flying from Umnak found the Japanese and attacked with torpedoes. For the third time that day the bombers scored no hits.

Untouched, the Japanese fleet steamed west. To the south of the chain they stood ready to defend the landing forces bringing soldiers to occupy Kiska and Attu. After the final B-26 attack the Americans lost contact with the carrier force until it returned to Japan. The troops and ships of the Japanese occupation force were discovered on Kiska Island by a patrolling PBY on June 8, initiating the next phase in the Aleutian Campaign.

Above, a B-17 Flying Fortress begins its takeoff between a PBY and P-40, Cold Bay.
Right, B-17s fuel up on the airfield, Cold Bay.

KISKA BLITZ

INSTRUCTIONS
TO BE FILLED OUT BY UNIT COMMANDER IMMEDIATELY UPON LANDING AFTER EACH ACTION OR OPERATION IN CONTACT WITH THE ENEMY.

DO NOT GUN DECK THIS REPORT-IF DATA CAN NOT BE ESTIMATED WITH REASONABLE ACCURACY ENTER A DASH IN SPACE FOR WHICH NO DATA IS AVAILABLE.

1. DATE June 10-14 1942   LAT. 52-57 LONG. 177-36   TIME Daylight Hours

2. WEATHER Overcast with breaks over objective

3. UNIT REPORTING Patrol Squadron Forty-Three   TYPE PLANES
                                                       PBY-5

4. NATURE OF OPERATION
        Bombing enemy shipping and shore installations in Kiska Harbor.

5. SPECIFIC OBJECTIVE
        Cruisers, destroyers, transports, moored planes and shore installations

6. FORCES ENGAGED
                 OWN   ENEMY
                 12 PBYs   Twin-float and single float seaplane fighters.
                                              Light and heavy AA fire

7. TYPE OF ATTACK Approach at low altitude just above overcast and diving planes through holes
        in the clouds at specific objectives

8. ENEMY TACTICS
        Enemy set up heavy barrage of Anti-aircraft fire through the holes in the clouds, in which the PBYs were diving.
        Subjecting planes to light and heavy anti-aircraft fire from ships and ashore when below overcast.

9. BRIEF DESCRIPTION OF ACTION
        Each plane attacked singly, approaching from whichever direction afforded the greatest cloud coverage. When over the
        harbor, patrol planes were put into a dive and bombs dropped. A pullout was attempted at 500-1500 feet altitude and
        plane immediately sought coverage again in the clouds

10. WEAPONS EMPLOYED
        Planes employed depth bombs with nose fuse, 500 lb. Demolition bombs, and strafed with .50 and .30 caliber machine
        guns.
        Enemy employed .30 and ..50 caliber, 20 mm and 3 inch Anti-aircraft guns

11. EVASIVE ACTION EMPLOYED
        Planes sought protection in cloud cover as soon as attack was completed

12. AMMUNITION EXPENDED
        18 depth bombs
        58 demolition bombs 500 lbs.

13. RESULTS (CERTAIN)
        Damage to shore installations, destruction of three four-engine flying boats by bombs and strafing.
        Hit on CL with 500 lb. Bomb

    RESULTS (ESTIMATED)
        Hits or near misses on AP, AK, DD, 2CL and destruction of one more four-engine flying boat

(cont.)

14. DAMAGE TO OWN AIRCRAFT

One airplane and crew missing, believed shot down in enemy action, two planes badly damaged by enemy action, and subsequently destroyed at advanced base. Two men killed and one wounded in one plane, many bullet and shrapnel holes in tail and wings of remaining planes participating.

15. REMARKS

One plane returned with 200 holes, one engine shot out, one aileron gone. Enemy light anti-aircraft very accurate at low altitudes. Heavy anti-aircraft was not troublesome, unless course and speed were maintained for about one minute. A few enemy planes of the Nakajima 57 type on floats were encountered but made only half-hearted attacks from long range. One pilot after attacking a CL at low altitude and pulling back up into the clouds, was almost thrown on his back by a violent explosion. This was separate and distinct from the relative light shocks resulting from the proceeding explosions of the bombs hitting and is believed due to a delayed explosion of the cruiser as a result of a direct hit. Due to undetermined damage to his plane the pilot did not return to observe the results.

C.B. Jones
Lt. Cdr. USN
Commanding VP-43

KISKA ISLAND

As the Japanese fleet retired from its position southwest of Dutch Harbor, two more small groups of enemy ships headed towards the westernmost Aleutian Islands. Their mission was to put ashore landing forces and occupy Attu, Kiska and Adak. These were, essentially, the only islands with functional harbors. The plan was modified when the Japanese learned of the airbase at Umnak, and the Adak operation was canceled. On June 6th, Kiska was "invaded" by 1,250 Japanese soldiers. The next day a force of 1,143 men landed on Attu. Also that day, a group of six Japanese "Mavis" four-engine seaplanes arrived at Kiska Harbor.

BERING SEA

ATKA ISLAND   NAZAN BAY

AMLIA ISLAND

ADAK ISLAND

PACIFIC OCEAN

Above, lines of Japanese infantry advance toward the ten-man weather station on Kiska Island. Right, the Japanese equivalent of the PBY, a four-engine "Mavis" flying boat in Kiska Harbor.

PHOTO FROM JAPANESE FILM VIA NATIONAL ARCHIVES

Above, a "Mavis" as it looked to a PBY flying over Kiska Harbor. Left, a sea–level view of a "Mavis" flying boat.
PHOTO FROM JAPANESE FILM VIA NATIONAL ARCHIVES

In order to report the weather, several weather stations were set up on islands along the chain. This was the station on Kiska.

The captured weather team being searched by a Japanese Officer. One member of the team fled to hills, surviving a month before turning himself in to the enemy.
PHOTO FROM JAPANESE FILM VIA NATIONAL ARCHIVES

There were no American military units west of Umnak. The Navy had put a ten–man weather forecasting unit on Kiska in order to relate the west moving weather patterns to Umnak and Dutch. PatWing Four had also placed seaplane mooring buoys in the harbor in case they used Kiska as an outpost. On Attu there was an Aleut village with 44 inhabitants, including a non–Aleut couple, Charles and Etta Jones. All were captured (Charles Jones committed suicide on Attu) and sent to Japan in September. On June 10, several planes on routine reconnaissance flights flew over Kiska Harbor. Below they saw a large group of ships, the Japanese landing forces. When the ships were learned to be Japanese, an all–out effort to bomb them off the island began. This became known as the "Kiska Blitz." It only lasted a few days but was extremely hard on the men and machines of PatWing Four and the Army Air Forces.

Ed Froehlich VP-41

Early on the morning of the 10 June, 1942, the weather had improved with 1,500–foot broken overcast, Crew "E" in 41-P-9 were headed south out of Umnak, mission patrol and to find out why the weather station—ten men at Kiska—had sent no weather reports since 7 June. About one half hour out of Umnak we sighted a PBY and crew on the beach on the south end of Umnak Island or one of those smaller islands south of Umnak. It turned out to be Lt. Jg. Jep Johnson's plane and crew missing since 3 June. They had landed out of fuel and couldn't radio their position for the lack of electrical power, no fuel. Mr. Bowers wobbled the wings of 41-P-9 and had Sissenwood send a radio message back to headquarters at Umnak and Dutch of their location. The crew and the plane were recovered. Because of no word from them for seven days, headquarters thought they had been shot down.

We arrived at Kiska shortly before noon, circled out of gun range. We saw a small Jap gunboat about one mile out the entrance to Kiska Harbor. On the intercom I heard Mr. Bowers tell Mr. Dinsmore, "That little thing can't hurt us, lets take a look inside the Harbor." He dropped down to about 100 foot altitude, past North Head into the harbor, and they were there waiting for us. The Jap Task force opened up on us with everything but the kitchen sink. Ainscough my 2nd Mec was in the tower, the AOM 3/C man on the bow .30 cal, the 3d AMN was on the starboard .50 cal, I was on the port .50 cal. and Sissenwood was manning the tunnel .30 cal, 2nd radioman was on the radio.

Mr. Bowers blocked the throttles in a port climbing turn, the engines bellowing full power. Ainscough was screaming on the intercom, "They're shooting at us." I glanced up at the port

Japanese ships fire on a patrolling PBY as they approach Kiska.

engine, cowl flaps closed, I started yelling on the intercom, "Open the cowl flaps." When using full power on the P & W 1830-92 engines, flaps wide open are a must, or you might blow cylinder heads right and left. The flaps came open and we entered some low clouds and headed back up the chain over 50 miles before Sissenwood could raise headquarters at Umnak or Dutch Harbor by radio to let them know the Japs were landing in Kiska Harbor. We were not hit but those tracers were close.

When we discovered the Jap landing at Kiska Harbor, I saw a large semicircle of six or more destroyers at anchor and inside that semicircle were three large cruisers at anchor, none underway. All were blinking lights and smoke from their guns. Behind them anchored parallel to the shore were three large transports or troop ships, small boats were running between them and the shore. There were piles of equipment, etc. stacked. Men were all over the place but no trucks or tractors. This was all I saw in the very short time before we entered the clouds.

When we landed at Nazan Bay (Atka Island) there were 20 PBYs moored, loaded or loading with 1,000-lb. and 500-lb. bombs, beginning takeoffs, for the Kiska Blitz. Since 41-P-9, Crew "E" was not loaded with demolition bombs nor fueled, we lucked out and were sent on a lone mission to Kodiak, returning late on 12 June to Umnak. We were sent on night patrol, no bombs or fuel left at Nazan Bay, the "Kiska Blitz" was nearly over, 14 of the 20 PBYs were flyable, six were lost or riddled, non–flyable. A lot of good men were lost too.

Frank Browning VP-41

Capt. Gehres was an ex–fighter pilot. His aggressive training sometimes made him impatient with his lumbering PBYs. When Jim Bowers reported Jap warships and transports in Kiska Harbor, Gehres ordered all PBYs to start carrying bombs to Kiska and to "continue until no bombs or no PBYs remained." Admiral Nimitz, CinC Pacific Fleet in Honolulu, immediately overruled Gehres order, and told General Buckner he was authorized to relieve Gehres with any officer in his command. The General replied that he was well satisfied with Gehres services. Then Gehres sent a directive that all copies of these messages were to be destroyed. But the word leaked out, and morale was not enhanced.

Bill Thies VP-41

There was a ten–man weather post on Kiska, before the invasion. We had not heard from them for several days, so I was ordered out there to see what might have happened to them. We

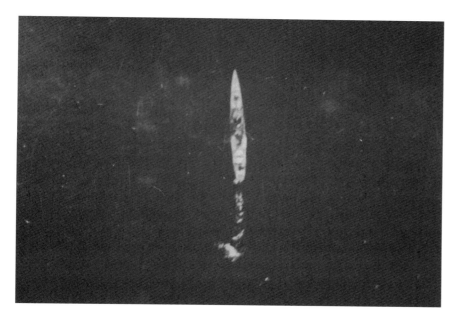

A Japanese warship heads out of Kiska Harbor as PBYs attack, June 18th.

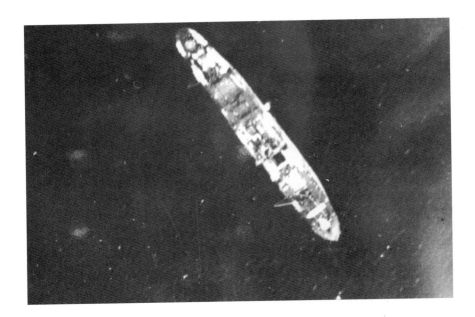

A Japanese transport in Kiska Harbor as seen from a PBY overhead.

were flying under about a 500–foot fog bank as we approached Kiska when we saw the invasion fleet and immediately took cover in the fog. We got as close as we dared and ducked in and out of the fog to get a count of the number and type of the ships to send the contact and amplifying reports.

After I sent my contact and amplifying messages to the wing commander, Leslie Gehres in Kodiak, and we turned east about 60 miles from Kiska, my radioman, Harvey, (who was either half soused or recovering from a hangover, but a hell of a radioman) approached me in the pilot's seat with a drawn .45 in one hand and a radio message in the other, and said—I will never forget his words—"You aren't going to do this, are you?" The message was in plain language, addressed to my personal call sign and read, "Bomb enemy shipping in harbor!" With the able assistance of my navigator, Bob Larson, we made, to the best of my knowledge, the first radar bombing ever attempted, and scored a hit on a troop transport amidst heavy AA fire.

Bob Larson VP-41

That morning we loaded up with four 500–pound GP bombs and flew to Kiska Harbor to investigate. Ensign James Bowers had reported unidentified ships in the harbor, but that was all the information we had. The weather was pretty much in our favor. A dense layer of clouds lay around Kiska, with a ceiling of 1,000 feet and around 2,000 or 3,000 feet thick. Between Umnak and 60 miles east of Kiska the clouds were broken and fairly good visibility prevailed. When we neared our objective we climbed over the clouds and flew the rest of the way on top. We let down about five miles east of the harbor and took a look. Half the Jap fleet (or so it seemed) was anchored in the harbor: two heavy cruisers, one light cruiser, five or six transports and about eight destroyers patrolling the nearby area. We studied them carefully from that distance through the binoculars and sent in a contact report, using the regular contact pad.

Then Thies climbed up on top of the clouds and spent the good part of an hour observing the situation through holes in the overcast. There were several thin spots directly over the harbor, and we kept skirting them, occasionally drawing anti–aircraft fire from the ships below. The clouds kept closing the hole over, and finally we lost it. Thies finally decided to let down a few miles east of the harbor, but when we broke through underneath we found ourselves right over the north side of the harbor. AA really started to break loose then. In addition to the fleet there were several flying boats—four–engine Mavises—tied to our own U.S. buoys. Thies poured on the coal, and we climbed back up into the clouds, and finally broke out on top again.

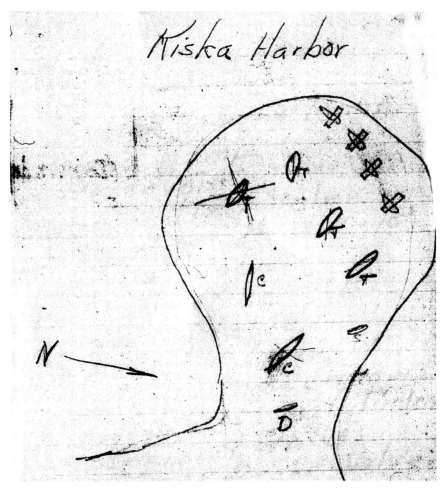

Kiska Harbor

N →

June 11 and 12, 1942

4 distroyers
2 cruisers
4 transports
4 patrol planes (Dummi
1 submarine

Al Knack, a crewman on PPC Bill Theis' PBY sketched these notes over Kiska Harbor. Knack kept extensive notes on all aspects of the Wing and his missions.

For the bombing run it was decided to set the interval-o-meter and release the bombs in a run right across the middle of the harbor, trusting luck to hit something. We flew right over some holes during the run and drew our heaviest AA then. Bill Lohse had the bomb release switch and was to pickle off the bombs.

The dialogue went something like this:

Thies said to Lohse: "I guess this is as good a place to drop the bombs as any"

Lohse: "What?"

Thies: "I said, drop the bombs."

Lohse: "You mean you want me to drop the bombs right now?"

Thies: (Well irritated by now) "Yes! Yes!"

Drop them he did. One bomb stuck on and was released manually. We went below to investigate. One of the bombs had hit a transport. Smoke was issuing from it in great amounts, and the Japs were attempting to maneuver it away from the rest of the fleet. As far as I know that was the first bombing of Kiska Harbor, and we were the first on the spot after Bower's incomplete report. After much pleading from the crew, Thies finally headed for home.

A Japanese transport burns in Kiska Harbor, June 18th, after being hit by bombs from a PBY. In all seven cargo ships, one destroyer and one submarine were destroyed by air attacks, Army and Navy, in Kiska Harbor.

We were almost to our mooring base at Atka when received orders to proceed to Kanaga and pick up the weather station personnel. The place was reported to have been captured by the Japs, so we were pretty cautious. It took some time to find the harbor, and after circling a few times to determine whether or not it was in enemy hands, we landed. To our relief the Japs hadn't landed, but the weathermen had hidden, thinking we were the Japs. By means of a couple of small boats their gear was transferred to the plane, and we took off in an evening that was fast growing dark. We set the dock on fire with a couple of gunnery runs, igniting the gasoline drums stored there.

It was nearly midnight by the time we reached Nazan Bay at Atka. So many other planes were moored in the bay we had difficulty in finding a spot to get tied up. We finally moored to a buoy and went aboard the aircraft tender USS Gillis *to get some rest.*

Although the weathermen were extremely happy to be evacuated, they were in misery for most of the flight. They were not accustomed to flying and all got very air sick. The disposal bags were in constant use. I remember one of them found a spot near my station at the navigation table and spent the entire trip leaning over a pail. I saw the same fellow a few years later at Adak, and he was still expressing his gratitude.

Bob Larson VP-41

About ten o'clock that morning (June 11th) the Gillis *loaded us up with four 500–lb. GPs, and we set out for Kiska again. Conditions were very much like the day before with an overcast at 1,000 feet with occasional clear areas. One of the clear areas unfortunately lay directly east of Kiska and spoiled our original plan of a timed bombing run from the tip of Little Kiska Island.*

We were about 20 miles east of Kiska at 800 feet when one of their four–engine Mavises sighted us and gave chase. In spite of their extra two engines, they were only slightly faster than us, and Thies eluded them easily by turning north and circling up through the clouds. For some reason the Japs seldom chased anyone through instrument weather. When we got on top, a twin–float seaplane (a Jake) was waiting for us. He seemed very reluctant to attack, and we took our own sweet time. We headed for Kiska Volcano, which stuck out above the clouds, snow covered sides gleaming in the sun. We planned another timed run from there.

Finally the Jap Jake started in on a run on us. We dove back into the "soup," circled the volcano on the bottom to the east side. We sighted a prominent landmark and started another timed run from there. The bottom of the overcast was very uneven, varying from low at our starting point to high over the target. We must have been in sight more than we expected due to the holes and the unevenness of the cloud bottom.

The next three minutes dragged by like hours, or so it seemed at the time. Like the day before, the overcast thinned out over the harbor, and we caught plenty of AA, mostly light automatic stuff. I was copilot that day and had the honor of pickling off the bombs. Again, our starboard, outboard bomb stuck on. Then Thies spotted one of their cruisers below us, put the plane in a steep dive, and manually released the remaining bomb.

The tracer shells of the AA were thick by that time, and we lost no time in heading for the clouds again. We did not see the bomb hit, but Knack, our plane captain, followed the bomb down as far as possible and swears it was headed directly for the cruiser. His observation point was the engine control tower, a good place to see anything happen. Wahl, on one of the waist 50s, managed to get in a few seconds of strafing the cruiser's decks.

We let down again east of the harbor to get a look. Low hanging clouds completely obscured the harbor, so we headed back for Dutch Harbor. We arrived with no further mishap.

A PBY flies low over the smokestack of a Japanese ship.
PHOTO FROM JAPANESE FILM VIA NATIONAL ARCHIVES

L.d. Campbell VP-41*

June 12th

Took off in Dutch Harbor with 4 bombs, 1,150 gallons gasoline at 0300 for Kiska. Attempted to locate harbor and GILLIS at Atka on trip out, but weather did not permit. Investigated grass fire at weather station on Kanaga encountered 2 single float bi-plane seaplanes. Avoided these by cloud flying, 3/4 hours later got on top at 11,000 feet. When gasoline reached 500 gallons, abandoned mission and set a course for Atka. Atka was closed in after repeated attempts to locate the harbor and set a course for Dutch Harbor. Arrived Dutch Harbor with all bombs aboard and 80 gallons gasoline.

June 13th

Took off from Otter Point at 2230 with 4 bombs, 1,300 gallons gasoline. Arrived Kiska at 0340 in the morning of June 14th. Overcast covered the island, but one peak of a volcano extended up out of the clouds. After rendezvous with volcano peak, made 4-minute run on course 174 degrees magnetic, then released 4 bombs in ripple salvo one second apart at 3,500 feet altitude. No AA fire, no planes sighted, result not observed. Returned to Dutch Harbor without any incident.

En. Leo Nuss VP-42*

– Kiska

Counted 6-8 ships—believe 1 CA, 5 DD possibly remains of wrecked vessels inshore. Approached from Kiska Volcano, crossed harbor at 3,000 feet. Released 4 bombs in ripple salvo. Waist gunner said one hit in a camp others in harbor—bombed through the fog and cloud.

Left Dutch Harbor armed with four 500–lb. bombs 0300 (plus 10)—landed at Atka took on 300 gallons gasoline. Went south of islands 50 miles. Landfall on Amchitka—north to Semisopochonol, west to Kiska Volcano. Bombed on course 130 (T). Icing at 4,000 feet.

After bombing course south of islands, but in sight contact with islands. Large grass fire on Cape Tusik, Kanaga Island, but no personnel visible. No activity noted on south side of island.

-Landed at Atka returning at about 1915, 12 June.

-Landed at Umnak about 2300 refueled to 800 gallons.

*From VP-42 War Diary

The planes and crews of VP-41 and VP-42 were worn thin. In an effort to bolster their numbers, the Navy assigned more PBYs to the Aleutians. Six planes from VP-51 were diverted from Hawaii. They flew many missions over Kiska and operated for two months from Sand Point. Another PatWing 4 squadron, VP-43, was flown up from the West Coast. They came up in three flights of four planes and stopped off in Kodiak, then Cold Bay or Dutch Harbor and from there headed straight for Nazan Bay on Atka, 360 miles away from Kiska. There the U.S.S. *Gillis* seaplane tender was waiting to service them. They landed, rested and began flying bombing missions to Kiska.

Oden Shepard VP-43

VP-43 left San Diego in June right after Dutch Harbor was bombed. We spent the night in Seattle, Sitka and Kodiak. Right after we arrived at Dutch Harbor, we fueled and loaded bombs. We then took off for Kiska and bombed it through the clouds. None of the planes were lost. One plane was hit pretty badly, and two men were killed. The two men who were killed were E.J. Keith and W.H. Sansing; that was June 11, 1942. Sansing was the plane captain, and Keith was the second mech. In another plane, during that first raid, a CPO was shot in the leg.

70

A bomb dropped from a PBY explodes near a Japanese ship.
PHOTO FROM JAPANESE FILM VIA NATIONAL ARCHIVES

Ed Froehlich VP-41

On to Attu, we flew over VP-43, commanded by Lt. Cdr. C.B. "Doc" Jones, with 12 new PBYs fresh out of the lower 48, at anchor in Nazan Bay, nine- or ten-man crews all lined up on top of the wings of the PBYs waving their arms at us as we flew over at about 1,500 foot altitude. We knew then we were getting some help with the Aleutian situation.

John Rodgers VP-41

A PBY takes off from Nazan Bay alongside the U.S.S. *Casco.*

One day we were flying out of Dutch Harbor—we had gone out to Kiska to bomb—and the Japs sent a plane up—I think they called it a Rufe. It was a Zero float–plane, anyway, he got on our back in a blind spot there and started shooting at us. He killed a photographer that had just gone along for the ride. A couple of the other fellows got shot up a little bit but not bad. When we got back to Dutch Harbor we landed on the water, and the plane was leaking, so we practically crashed on to the beach, and water was just running out of the holes in the plane. I think we had 257 bullet holes in the plane. Of course, some of them were from the top and went all the way through.

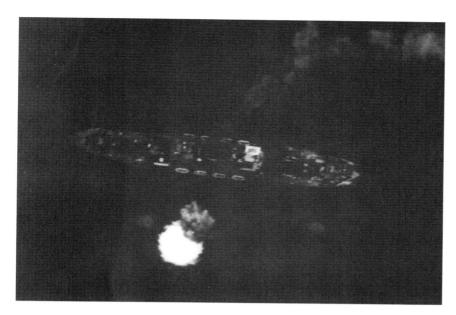

Two 500–lb. GP bombs straddle a Japanese transport in Kiska Harbor.

Ralph S. Erskine VP-41 (journal entries)

25 June 1942. Crosby (the photographer) was killed by a Japanese fighter plane that got underneath the tail of the PBY and shot up the area where the blisters were. Brooks Cumbie was in the same area, and he was shot up but not killed.

28 June 1942. Today I salvaged some radio equipment out of a wrecked plane. William J. Glover's plane and his crew are missing.

21 July 1942. We started attacking the Japanese at Kiska full scale. Some of the radiomen that were flying gave me their money to hold for them just in case they were shot down.

Bill Maris VP-43

We bombed ships in Kiska Harbor. I could see the tracer bullets / shells coming at us as we dove in releasing our bombs and pulling out. We were attacked by a single float–fighter on climb out. Got some hits / tracer on the fighter. The pilot just sat there and looked at us, then flipped it over to his port and dove into some cloud cover. We turned to Starboard and back into the clouds at about 2,000 ft. heading for home at Chernofski Harbor.

Rob Donley VP-42

During June of 1942, we began night bombing of Kiska. It was quite difficult to find the target as our navigation was by dead reckoning plus the assistance of a Scope Radar. The B-24 planes of the Army Air Force were also flying then. They had little experience in navigating Aleutian weather and often were lost, ditching in the Pacific Ocean. To assist them, one of our pilots was assigned as navigator on a B-24 bombing mission over Kiska. His name was Clark Hood, an academy graduate. The B-24 in which he was navigator was hit by anti–aircraft and went down in flames.

Bill Thies VP-41

We had no contact to speak of with Army Air. We operated VERY independently, except for the fact that none of the Army pilots or their crews knew how to navigate over water, so the Navy loaned out a lot of young officers who could help them find their way. The ones that were ordered to do that were very unhappy.

A PBY flys low and slow over Kiska, surrounded by AA bursts.

The same PBY explodes on the hillside after being shot down.

Bob Larson VP-41

We had some operations in Nazan Bay (Atka), because it was closer to Kiska targets than Umnak. One of the neat things about PBY-5A was its amphibious capability. By sending a couple of seaplane tenders into Nazan you would have an instant Naval Air Station for PBY seaplane operations. However, a PBY could take off with a heavier weight from a runway than it could with a water takeoff. As I recall, we took off fully loaded from Umnak, flew to Kiska for a bombing mission, then returned to Atka. There we would be rearmed with partial fuel for another Kiska mission.

We had two tenders that serviced us. One was the Williamson, *a converted WW I destroyer, and the other was the* Casco, *built from the keel up as a seaplane tender. One time when we approached the* Casco *to take on fuel, Thies got chewed out by one of the ship officers for some reason that I don't remember. Bill got so mad that after we tied up to a buoy, he refused to go on board the* Casco *for the night. The crew of the* Casco *were not very friendly. On board the* Williamson, *it was just the opposite. One of the shipboard officers let me use his bunk one night. When the* Casco *got torpedoed one day, we were glad it happened to them and not the*

A crew climbs aboard their PBY through the blister, Nazan Bay, Atka Island.

A PBY-5 of VP-43 sits in Nazan Bay. VP-43 flew up from San Diego after the attacks on Dutch Harbor. They arrived just in time to bomb Kiksa as part of the "Blitz." VP-51 also came north at this time.

Williamson. *The* Casco *was beached and repaired later.   These were relatively short–lived operations. Later in the war an airfield was built at Atka, but I never landed there.*

Bill Thies VP-41

The night we landed in Nazan Bay, we went astern of the Casco *to refuel. My copilot was a full lieutenant (Naval Academy), Peter F. Boyle. We called him "Peter the Fox." I was either a Lt. (Jg) at that time or a very junior Lt., so the Fox was senior to me. I had a firm understanding with Foley before he assigned the Fox to my crew, that I was in command of the PBY, Peter be damned! The skipper of the* Casco *was on the stern observing the refueling. I believe he was a full Commander.*

I had the torpedo and bomb on, so I knew my limitations of weight and balance for water takeoff and knew what fuel I needed to get to Kiska and back. When we took on what I needed, I told them to stop fueling. The Casco's *CO said he had orders to fuel me to full capacity. I told him in so many words to stick it in his ear. The Fox went crazy. He said you can't talk to a full Commander like that. Then the* Casco *CO ordered me aboard. I refused and told him I was* starting engines, going to anchor buoy and give the crew some rest. Boyle opened his hatch and tried to get out. I pulled him back down and told him to sit and shut up! That was that. Never heard anymore about it.

Frank Browning VP-41

Bill Thies took some kidding about his box of cigars from Capt. Gehres. In early August, Adm. Smith scheduled a bombardment of Kiska with his cruisers and destroyers. VP-41 was directed to provide air support in case enemy carriers showed up. We flew out to Kiska in two three–plane sections, with each PBY carrying a torpedo under one wing. LCDR, Foley had the first section and was fueled and armed first. I had Thies and three others for wingmen, and we were about an hour behind. Kiska was fogged in. I learned later the ships finally found a clear spot and started firing blind about 8PM. They dumped 400 tons of steel and TNT on Kiska in the next 20 minutes then withdrew. I wish we could have seen the show. We slopped around the area until daylight got short, but no one asked for our help, and we headed back. Foley's group had started back earlier and were able to reach our tender in Nazan Bay before dark. At dusk we had to land at Amchitka, about 75 miles east of Kiska. I sent a status report to Dutch Harbor and told them not to wait up. Before landing, Jim Bowers and I each jettisoned our torpedo, as had all of Foley's section, Bill Thies elected to keep his. Landing with a one–ton torpedo hanging under one wing is not too difficult in good conditions, but it's not something we practice. The water was not rough, and Thies did a good job, as usual. Capt. Gehres was delighted to get his torpedo back, and gave him a box of cigars.

Bill Thies VP-41

The operations in Nazan Bay lasted quite awhile, but I don't remember just how long. If I had to guess, I would say two

PPC Bill Theis with one of the cigars given to him for landing with a 2,000–lb. torpedo. There were precious few torpedoes in the Aleutians, and it was so difficult to land carrying one they were usually jettison prior to coming in.
PHOTO VIA B. THEIS

or three weeks. I think I only made two or three sorties in and out of there. The reason for operating from there was that it put us a lot closer to Kiska, therefore quicker turnaround time and less fuel. That was the period when we were trying to bomb the Japanese off of Kiska.

We never went ashore nor aboard the DH (seaplane tender). We "lived" in the PBYs. One hellish night like only the Aleutians can produce, we found our way through the narrow entrance to Nazan Bay by radar. I had a torpedo and a 500–lb. bomb under the wings. I should have dropped them if I had any sense, but that meant we would have to spend hours reloading them. We were operating on a continuous turn around with no rest breaks. We landed just after we got inside the bay, because I knew there were lots of high rocks, and we were flying at about 50 feet off the water.

A PBY refueling off the *Casco*.

I broke radio silence and asked for help to find my way to the Casco. *No response. I didn't know it at the time, but the* Casco *had taken a Japanese submarine torpedo and had beached to keep from sinking, and the submarine was still in the bay. (One of our PBYs sank it the next day) I kept yelling on the radio and said, "This is Bill Thies, for Christsake, somebody turn on a searchlight, so I will know where I'm at!"*

Norm Garton was the skipper of the destroyer that was in the bay, and that was the ship I nearly bombed on Dec 7th. He heard my plea and took the gamble of turning on his searchlight and exposing his ship to another torpedo attack. He lit up the Casco *briefly then turned off the light. I was able to tie up to the* Casco's *stern and refuel. Not having to load bombs and torpedoes gave my crew a much-needed rest for a few hours.*

All during WWII, I smoked cigars. Gehres, knowing that, gave me a box. On the cardboard cover, he wrote "For Lt. Bill Thies, my personal decorations for bringing back the torpedo and bomb. L. Gehres, Capt. USN, CPW-4." I have cherished that piece of cardboard all these years

Sam Cobean VP-43

As you know, the native residents of Atka were evacuated to the mainland in mid June '42, aboard the USS Gillis. *The powers that be knew that the meager defenses available for the chain had no chance of stopping a major Japanese invasion force, certainly not w sest of Dutch Harbor.*

The village was torched to deny the enemy anything useful. As I remember, one or two houses were relatively habitable, the rest mostly rubble including the beautiful church, the destruction of which brought much anguish to all of us. The hulk of one of our planes, battle-damaged from Kiska bombing, was on the beach facing the church ruins.

On about the 20th of August, VP-43 was operating from the USS Casco, *anchored in Nazan Bay between Atka and Amelia Islands. Non-flying planes were moored to buoys along a curved section of beach adjacent to the village. Myself, Don Long and one or two others were doing maintenance and re-arming on an aircraft buoyed a couple of miles from the ship.*

I was working on the bow turret gun and had just loaded it, when I saw a twin-float enemy plane approaching, almost overhead, flying toward Casco. *I immediately commenced firing, and in 30 seconds or so—seemed like an hour—* Casco's *AA batteries opened up. The intruder turned west and departed the area. I saw a piece fall from the target but must assume that the hit was not lethal.*

The ship slipped anchor immediately, got under way and departed the area, leaving us to our own devices. We decided that to stay on the plane (1,800 gals of fuel) was not prudent, as the bogie had seen Casco *depart and would surely return for strafing runs, so we went ashore (in*

Above, a Japanese observation plane photographed PatWing 4 ships and planes in Nazan Bay, Atka Island. Right, small boats ferry crews to their planes in Nazan Bay.
PHOTO VIA UNALASKA HISTORICAL COMMISSION

a life raft or service boat). We reconnoitered the village, and since we had no idea how long our stay on the island would be, we started collecting items for defense and survival—shelter, food, cooking gear, etc. The small stream by the village was literally bank to bank with salmon. Since I had never seen a salmon run and had no idea how long this phenomenon would last, I waded into the stream and commenced throwing fish onto the bank like there was no tomorrow—100 or so just in case.

We had noticed several chickens about, and after several meals of boiled, broiled, steamed, etc. salmon only, a pot of chicken would be a delicious change. We found a large pot and proceeded to cook our dream meal. Almost immediately a very unappetizing aroma made it evident that something wasn't right. Our dream meal turned out to be awful. It seems that the chickens had nothing to eat for two months but rotten salmon, and that's exactly how it tasted. I believe that a ship or plane picked us up on the forth or fifth day.

Robert Brown VP-42

Flying in and around Kiska was always a little scary. Not knowing what to expect, always keeping cover if needed. Sometimes we carried bombs, depth charges or torpedoes.

One time we spent the night in our plane at base while they tried to attach a torpedo to our plane so in the morning we could go at a freighter that just arrived in Kiska Bay. I didn't sleep any that night, I'm sure I said my prayers a few times. They couldn't get it attached, so they sent out some Army bombers, and they found out the freighter was heavily armed.

Flying in the Aleutians made me think a lot about life. I had letters made out to my sister and friends in my locker, in case of not returning, especially in the month of June, when you went out not knowing what you were going to run into. It was sorta spooky. Outside of losing my first crew, flying in and around Kiska and being lost, very bad weather made a believer out of me. I gave my thanks every night for another day to fly. I can't say I was really scared but so wanted to return home some days. I felt so bad for the loss of our shipmates.

A camouflaged Japanese ships sits in Kiska harbor as AA fire fills the sky around an attacking PBY.

THE AKUTAN ZERO

In July 1940, the Japanese produced the first Zero fighter. It was used against China with overwhelming results. In fact, the early reports of its performance were disregarded by the U.S. military as impossible. That opinion changed after Pearl Harbor, December 7, 1941 and successive air battles over the next six months. In the Pacific Theater, great distances made the time a plane could fly as important as speed and agility. The Zero fighter (named by the Americans the "Zeke") combined all these characteristics, making it unmatched in combat for the first two years of the war. None of the American fighter planes could out–fly the Zero, and most dogfights were very one–sided. The Americans were desperate to learn the characteristics of the plane in order to develop tactics to defeat it. At Pearl Harbor, a few Zeros were shot down, but little could be learned from the wreckage.

On a routine patrol July 9, 1942, a PBY from VP-41 got blown several hundred miles off course. When they were returning one man saw a plane lying in the tundra on Akutan Island, less than 40 miles from Dutch Harbor. It turned out to be a Japanese Zero, which crashed there a month before, a victim of anti–aircraft fire over Dutch. While many crews had seen the plane, it was Bill Thies and crew who convinced their commander that they should check it out.

Bill Thies VP-41

Until the Japanese invaded Kiska, we had a weather station out there. Beings that weather moves from west to east, they were able to furnish some very rough information. Other than

This extraordinary sequence shows a Zero hit by AA fire over Dutch Harbor. This is most likely the plane which crashed on Akutan, 30 miles east of Dutch Harbor.

that, with no radio aids or satellites we were generally in the dark about weather. Our fore-caster was a Commander John Tatum. He was as good as there was. I relied on his forecasts and owed my life to him on many occasions. But, with not very much info to go on, he was often wrong.

The incident of the Zero discovery was due to a mistake he made, calling for winds from the east when they turned out to be about 60 knots from the west, which caused us to end up at Akutan instead of Adak. One night, our C.O. Paul Foley got me out of bed. It was my turn for a day off. The weather was so horrible that the "ready" crews refused to fly. Foley said that if I would go first the rest of the crews would follow.

I told my radioman/radarman to let me know after we got enough altitude to clear some mountains on Adak and passed a certain point of land. After getting to altitude and turning south I waited and waited for Harvey (that was his name) to notify me so we could start our navigation.

Finally I got on the intercom and asked him if there was a problem. He told me that we were over the point but the radar showed we had been over the point for about ten minutes. I went back and looked at the screen myself, and the blip wasn't changing. I got my copilot on the intercom (I think it was Larson) and told him to do a 180. He did and the blip went off the screen at 210 knots! We had a head wind of 105 knots! To do the search, we "crabbed."

It was on this mission that after 14 hours the radar did not pick up any land at 50 miles. I had no idea where we were, so we landed in the open sea to save gas and try to figure out where we were. After bobbing around in 30–foot seas for about an hour, the fog broke enough that Larson got a sun sight with the sextant, which showed we were still a 100 miles south of the chain, but we didn't know our longitude.

We took off and to make a long story short, when we hit the chain we identified that we had been blown eastward off course the distance between Adak and Akutan. That is when we discovered the Zero and landed at Dutch.

Bob Larson VP-41

I was the second pilot of Bill Thies' PBY crew during the early phase of the Aleutian War. It was about five weeks or so after the Dutch Harbor raids, and things had calmed down a bit. We were doing a routine search patrol south of Dutch Harbor.

Our searches were timed so as to be out at the maximum distance from Dutch at about daybreak. This meant taking off at dusk and flying all night. It is pertinent to mention that at that time there were no radio aids to navigation in the Aleutians. Twenty–three range stations were installed later, but that didn't do us much good then. Navigation at night in the Aleutians was complicated by the perpetual clouds that made it impossible to see stars. One could get a drift angle and calculate the effect of the wind, if one were low enough to the water. Most of the PBYs tried to stay in sight of the water to make a more effective search. If low clouds prevented this, we would fly on top and make a pure radar search. The old "A" scope radar we had was not very reliable, and a visual search was encouraged.

To determine drift angle caused by the wind at night, you could drop a smoke float. When it hit the water the flare would ignite, and you could take a bearing on it with a pelorus. For some reason which seems strange to me now, we were ordered not to drop smoke floats on the theory that we would give away our position to the enemy, as if the noise of the PBY weren't enough. On that night, a 100% overcast was above us. We were heading into a rather deep, low–pressure area south of Dutch.

Bill Lohse was navigating that night, and I got a chance to be copilot. Our practice was to make an estimate from the state of the sea before it got totally dark. After flying for several hours in the murk, we would get another estimate of the wind in the dawn's early light, and make a guess as when the wind shifted during the night. On that particular search, the wind was from the east just at dusk, so we corrected our course to the east.

It was a rough and dark night, no stars were visible, and we were navigating on dead reckoning alone using an unknown wind. Came the dawn, and we noted that now the wind was very strong and coming from the west. How long it had been doing that was anybody's guess. We corrected course for the new wind and wondered how far off course we were.

We were an hour overdue to see any landmarks. Thies was understandably getting pretty worried. Radar then being somewhat unreliable, there was a possibility that we had crossed the Aleutians during the night and were headed north into the vast Bering Sea. Finally, the sun rose a few degrees, so I took a sextant shot of it. It was really too low for accuracy, but I felt the answer was worth something. The sextant read more than four degrees higher than I calculated. This meant we were probably more than 240 nautical miles to the east of our course.

Assuming the "shot" was correct, this accounted for the long overdue landmark, since the chain is much further north at the eastern end. In another 15 minutes—to our great relief—we sighted distant mountains, which later proved to be the Shumagin Islands. The weather improved considerably, and we could actually fly over some of the islands on the way home, instead of skirting them along the shoreline.

The Zero as it lay undisturbed in the tundra. The large white piece is an external fuel tank ripped off the bottom of the plane.

The two ruts made by the extended landing gear of the Zero can be seen filled with water. The gear was ripped off and the plane flipped, killing the pilot.

While passing over Akutan Island, just to the east of Dutch, one of the gunners reported seeing an airplane flat on its back on the tundra below. (The gunner was George Raptist, an enlisted pilot, who was sick from the rough air and was vomiting out of the gun blister when he got the first look at the downed Zero.) We passed directly over it. Thies banked, the airplane around and descended to have a look. The downed plane was upside down, but didn't look too badly damaged. We marked the position on a map and went in to Dutch.

Bob Larson VP-41

We were released from patrol duty by the skipper and told to start salvage work on the plane. We got aboard a YP boat—a converted fishing, boat used for patrol purposes—and proceeded to Akutan. We were warned that Japanese crews might still be around and to advance cautiously. We got to the beach and hiked in, all armed to the teeth. (I had a Thompson submachine gun). We approached cautiously in a slough, standing in about a foot of water, through which grass was growing. From the air, the ground looked like a meadow, and the Japanese

The body of the pilot, Tadayoshi Koga, before it was buried.

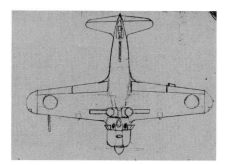

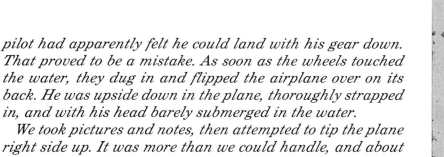

pilot had apparently felt he could land with his gear down. That proved to be a mistake. As soon as the wheels touched the water, they dug in and flipped the airplane over on its back. He was upside down in the plane, thoroughly strapped in, and with his head barely submerged in the water.

We took pictures and notes, then attempted to tip the plane right side up. It was more than we could handle, and about the best we could do was prop the tail up so we could get the pilot and his gear out. We also removed the 20mm Oerlikon guns out of the wings. It was a mighty impressive piece of equipment. Our gunner had no trouble field-stripping it. We accused him of getting his early training with the Japanese Navy.

We were rather surprised at the details. It was a well built airplane. We could only see one bullet hole in it in the vicinity

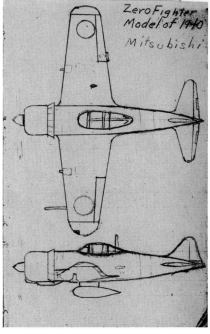

Al Knack, who helped spot the Zero, drew these sketches on the first trip in case on one ever went back.

The tail of the plane was lifted to gain access to the cockpit. Note the water soaked ground.

Bill Theis, Bob Larson and their crew swarm over the Zero.

Loading the Zero for transport to San diego.

of the oil cooler. The pilot had a parachute and life raft, somewhat discrediting the theory that Japanese pilots weren't interested in survival. We could find no sword.

The plane had simple, unique features. Inspection plates could be opened by pushing on a black dot with a finger. A latch would open and one could pull the plate out. I kept one for a souvenir, figuring the Navy could build a replacement later. The wing tips folded by unlatching them and pushing them up by hand.

As luck would have it, that was the first Japanese Zero fighter captured in the war. Later, a more professional salvage crew recovered it and sent it to San Diego on a ship. There it was rebuilt and test flown to get data.

I guess if we hadn't got lost that night, we may not have recovered that Zero. You couldn't see it from the usual PBY route nor from a ship deck. The plane got good press. Life *magazine featured an article on it, and the incident has appeared in various books on the Aleutian war, the Zero fighter, and elsewhere.*

Bill Thies lead a salvage crew to Akutan and discovered they could not move the plane, but that the plane was in good enough shape to make recovery worthwhile. It took two more salvage attempts before the plane was put on a sled and brought down to the beach and shipped to Dutch. The engine was removed and moved separately.

At Dutch, guards were posted to make sure no GIs took any vital parts as souvenirs. 7.7mm machine gun bullets were the most popular items grabbed as trophies by the guys working on plane.

After three attempts, a sled was built, and the plane was dragged to a ship and ferried to Dutch Harbor. Here it is being crated, then loaded onto a transport to be delivered to San Diego.

From Dutch the plane was shipped to N.A.S. San Diego, fixed up and reflown in September 1942. Its performance was evaluated, weaknesses noted and was test flown against most of the current American fighters. The information was sent out to all fighter units and is credited with saving many lives.

Anyone interested in learning more about the Zero found on Akutan should read Jim Reardon's excellent book, *Koga's Zero: The Fighter That Changed WWII*.

EVACUATION OF THE ATKA ALEUTS

When the Japanese were discovered on Kiska and Attu, it presented a strange dilemma for the U.S. military. The village of Attu was in enemy hands, which made the Village of Atka and its 83 Aleuts the nearest people to the Japanese–held areas. Would they be next? A decision was made to evacuate these people without much thought as to next step. The PBYs were operating off of Nazan Bay where the village was located. Also in the bay were a succession of seaplane tending ships.

Bob Spence VP-41

For their safety, the Aleut people were ordered to disperse to their summer fish camps. On June 12th, the two white schoolteachers left on the USS Gillis. That same day the village was

The village of Atka on Nazan Bay. Its 100 residents lived by fox farming, sealing and subsistence. The building in the foreground is the Russian Orthodox Church.

ordered burned to deny its use to the enemy. Another seaplane tender, USS Hulbert *collected the Aleuts in preparation to evacuate them. Because of the dispersal, 21 people did not come to the ship. The ships left them behind. Two days later, two PBYs were ordered to collect the last group and fly them to Dutch Harbor. The pilot of the airplane that day was Lloyd Carpenter, long time Aleutian flyer, and two PBYs from VP-41 went in to bring the remainder of the people at Atka out. A destroyer had picked up everyone else, and there was, to the best of my remembrance, about 30 people left there, and we each took half of them.*

We had the chief of the village and his daughter in our airplane, and the daughter had been out to school at some time, and she spoke quite good English, which was a great help to us. Hardly any of them spoke English; even the chief spoke very little English, but the daughter made a great interpreter. She was a bright girl. She would have been a teenager. It was an experience for us, but I'm sure it was an experience for them, because they came out in their boats, and they all had some bundles of things which we had to tell them that they couldn't take with them. We had quite a load to take off on the water. By that time we had 15-20 people in there with our nine–man crew. So we got all loaded up, so they just turned their boats loose. There was no other thing to do with them. All out in the middle of the bay. They wanted to bring guns and other things. There was a great amount of things in the boat that we just wouldn't let them bring it on.

The other airplane took off, and we took off. The water was pretty rough, and because of the big load we had to run and smash through the water for awhile—like a PBY does—before we got flying, and they were frightened, of course. I thought they handled it pretty well for a first flight. Once we became airborne and smoothed out, leveled off, then they all figured they were gonna live, and they became pretty cheerful.

In the meantime, the crew had been running back and forth with buckets, because a lot of them got airsick before we got airborne, but the Chief was very stoic, he and the little girl, she had done just great. It was a little crowded in there, particularly when they started throwing up.

When we got going good, Carpenter let the chief come up and sit in the copilot seat for awhile and oh, he thought that was great. He could look around. He went by the Islands of Four Mountains—I remember in particular he knew what that was. He recognized that from the air.

When we arrived at Dutch Harbor, the two airplanes and we unloaded all these people. It looked like they were just coming out like people coming out of a funny car at a circus. Just went on and on and on, and there was the other airplane with the same amount. So we had quite a crowd by the time that was over, and then from that point on, people came in and took care of them. But they had gone around and shook hands with the crew and thanked them to the best of their ability. It was an unusual flight—even for us in a PBY.

We found out then that there was an attempt made shortly after that to burn the village, so that the Japanese wouldn't have the use of it. I understood that the first burn didn't burn so much. I saw it after that, and it wasn't completely burned down. We operated on that vehicle two or three different times. Eventually they did get it burned down.

87

Ed Froehlich VP-41

41-P-9 Crew "E" landed at deserted Nazan Bay. Buildings ashore still burning and smoking, and picked up the remaining natives, 21 Aleut men and boys, their rifles, slicker bags, etc., all smelling like fish and flew them to Dutch Harbor. With 30 men and a lot of luggage, Mr. Bowers (pilot) decided to dump some spare fuel (I always carried 100 extra gallons for Grandma.) Dumping 300 gallons was hair–raising, the drainpipe leading from the starboard—unsealed fuel tank dump valve to the trailing edge of the wing—leaked profusely. High octane gas running over a large portion of the lower side of the starboard wing and the side of the hull. One spark and we would have gone up with a bang. But luck was with us, all electrical units had been secured. We ticked along with the port engine into the wind 'til we got out of the gasoline slick. It took about five minutes. We started the starboard engine, and after one of the longest take off runs I ever made, we made it out the harbor into the swells finally, airborne and back to Dutch Harbor. The Jap bombers arrived (over Atka) about one or two hours after we had left.

To deny the buildings of Atka to the enemy, almost the entire village was burned.

Vern Monckton VP-41

One incident that I recall that has stuck in my mind was when one of our planes returned from evacuating an Aleut village. I don't recall how many people were in that plane, but it seemed like they would never quit getting out. Every man carried his rifle, if nothing else. I don't know if any one took a picture, but someone should have.

88

When the people returned to Atka, the government provided them with material to rebuild their homes.

The Aleut people from Attu were taken prisoner to Japan. After the war they were denied access to Attu and forced to relocate to Atka by the U.S. Government.

Happy to be back in their village, the inhabitants of Atka pose with Navy officers upon their return in 1945.

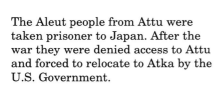

ANTI—SUBMARINE OPERATIONS

One of the important missions of Naval Patrol Planes was that of anti–submarine patrol. This was difficult in the Aleutians because of the low ceilings and perpetual whitecaps. Low ceilings did not allow a wide field of vision, and whitecaps made it very difficult to spot the white trail of a submarine periscope. However, sometimes PBYs were successful in their efforts to attack enemy subs. Sometimes they weren't.

Bob Larson VP-41, June 6, 1942

Our mission on this particular day was to search for and bomb a lone Japanese cruiser on which a couple of bearings had been taken by our monitors the night before. Four planes were assigned to this mission, all armed with SAPS—semi–armor piercing bombs. We all took separate areas to search. The crew that found the cruiser was to keep in contact with it until the rest arrived on the scene. We were then to bomb in formation from 10,000 feet.

We had been out for several hours in our sector, which took us westward along the islands. We got a radio message from the base directing us to torpedo an enemy group reported to be 35 miles north of Seguam Island. Since we had been previously ordered to arm with 500–lb. SAP bombs with instantaneous fuses, this was obviously impossible, but with PatWing Four this was a typical order—fouled up as usual.

Our ship was lead plane, so we sent out a message ordering all planes to rendezvous over Seguam, formate, then proceed on to the target position to bomb it. We didn't want to waste time returning to the base to change to torpedoes. (Given a choice, bombing is safer).

We arrived over Seguam and circled for an hour, but none of the other planes appeared. It was decided to attack alone, so we headed north to the reported position of the enemy fleet. In addition to the regular crew we had Chief Ordinanceman Anderson with us to operate the bombsight. He was in the bow compartment during most of the trip.

We searched for quite a while from 10,000 feet over a solid overcast, depending entirely on radar to pick up the fleet. We went down beneath the overcast and searched some more. The clouds hung very low—about a 300-foot ceiling. We gave up the search below, went on top, and started for home.

Half an hour later, Harvey, our radioman, called up on the inter-phone saying there was an object on the radar scope four miles away. He homed in on it and passed directly over it. We had several similar indications that day which proceeded to be rocks, so we weren't very eager to investigate. We turned 180 degrees, kept this course for several minutes, then resumed our original course to pass over the spot again. We picked up the target again and went below to investigate. The ceiling below was ragged, and varied from 2-300 feet. Visibility was about one to two miles.

Suddenly we sighted a surfaced submarine, apparently charging its batteries, accounting for the fact that they hadn't heard us. We were practically unarmed. The 500-lb. bombs could not be dropped from lower than 750 feet with the fusing arrangement, without endangering our own airplane. The ceiling was so low we couldn't get up to that altitude. We headed for the sub anyhow, intending to strafe. Suddenly a sharp explosion changed the apparent situation.

Holes appeared all over the plane, and the starboard engine caught fire. Our first thought was that we had been hit with AA fire. We figured if the sub could do that much damage with one shot, it was not very prudent to let him have a second one. We immediately pulled up in the soup above us. The fire was put out with the CO2 system, and the engine feathered. The bombs were also jettisoned to reduce our weight. Shortly before they were dropped, we noticed that only three bombs were on the racks when there should have been four. When things calmed down a bit, we thought it over finally coming to the conclusion that we had dropped our own bomb! Anderson, in the heat of excitement, had selected a bomb and must have later stepped on the bomb release switch, unexpectedly dropping the bomb at a dangerously low altitude.

We flew back to Dutch Harbor on one engine and repaired the damage in flight the best way we could. The hull was full of holes of varying sizes. The large holes were plugged with rags and boards, while the small ones were stuffed with pencils and bits of wood. We all considered ourselves lucky to have come through without a scratch in the entire crew.

One piece had come through between the two pilots. The tunnel gunner had a piece of bomb come up right between his arms while he was holding the spade grips of the gun. (That was his last trip with our crew). The largest hole was made in the hull near the side wheel well, and measured about 12 inches long. We made a water landing at Dutch and taxied up to the ramp as fast as possible to avoid taking on too much water. We probably missed the sub completely.

Pat Wing 4 War Diary

June 12th
   USS GRANT sailing from Cold Bay beginning 0405. One plane
   Lt.jg Bergstrum, sighted a periscope off Sanak Island in 54°32' N–162°30' W
   An immediate attack was made dropping one depth bomb. No damage to the submarine
   was apparent, but an attack on the GRANT was probably averted.

A PBY drops a 350–lb. depth bomb
(file photo)

A submarine periscope as seen from
a PBY. PHOTO VIA H. FORT

Middle, a PBY approaching the
stern of the USS *Casco*.
Bottom, Nazan Bay, Atka Island in
winter. The village was located in
the cove on the left. The torpedoed
Casco was aground on the beach top
center.

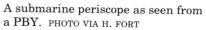

Below, one torpedo missed the *Casco*
and ran up on the sandy beach.
PHOTO VIA UNALASKA HISTORICAL
COMMISSION

After realizing his ship was sinking, the skipper ran her aground.

The hole in the side can be seen clearly. Two tugs try to pull her off the beach.

PPC Carl Amme's crew was given partial credit for the sinking of RO-61.

The submarines of WWII operated with two types of power. When submerged, the subs were driven by electric motors powered by batteries. When the batteries ran low, the boats surfaced and ran a diesel engine. This propelled the sub as well as recharged the batteries. When possible subs ran on the surface, which made them easy to spot. When recharging batteries they often tried to hide in the shadows of cliffs.

The sinking of RO-61 on August 31, 1942 was truly a success story of the men and machines of PatWing 4. The U.S.S. *Casco* was stationed, along with the U.S.S. *Williamson*, in Nazan Bay, Atka Island, to tender advanced elements of the wing. At this time, the Army was making landings on Adak Island with the goal of making it the next base in the advance towards Kiska. The PBYs were flying all over the chain doing anti–shipping patrols, convoy escorts and accompanying bombardment missions to Kiska.

In Nazan Bay with the two seaplane tenders was the destroyer U.S.S. *Reid*. The evening of August 29, the *Reid* left the harbor to take some Army engineers to Adak. Unknown to the Americans, a Japanese submarine had slipped into the bay that day and sat on the bottom waiting. When its batteries and air ran low the next night it surfaced. They believed that they were trapped by the destroyer in the bay. When they discovered the *Reid* gone, they fired both torpedoes at the *Casco* and raced from the harbor.

One torpedo missed the tender and slid up the smooth sand beach. The other hit the *Casco* amidships, killing five men and blowing a huge hole in her side. The ship was run up into the sand to keep it from sinking. One notable action aboard the *Casco* was by Aviation Ordinanceman Sam Cobean. When an automatic lifeboat flare ignited while floating in a slick of fuel, Cobean jumped in the frigid waters and held the flare underwater until it went out. He received the silver star for this.

A PBY in Nazan Bay passed the alert around the chain. PPC Amme took off from Dutch the next morning with medical supplies, and PPC Coleman flew in from Adak. On the north side of Atka, hidden in the shadow of a sea–cliff, was the RO-61, surfaced. Both planes saw it simultaneously and attacked.

Ernest "Dutch" Elisevier VP-43

When the Casco *was torpedoed, I was with a plane crew in Dutch Harbor to pick up some gear. VP-43 was based with* Casco *at that time. On our return to the* Casco, *we heard over the radio that the* Casco *was torpedoed, and on our way back we looked around to see if we could find the Japanese submarine. We spotted the sub and depth–charged her. There was also another plane flying with us that did some bombing. A destroyer came up and picked up some of the Japanese sailors. The sub was sunk. The* Casco *was patched up, went to the U.S. to be repaired and was put back into service again.*

Ray Falk VP-43

Lt. Dahl our regular PPC was recovering from a hernia operation in Dutch Harbor. Lt. Dahl had an emergency hernia attack and was sent to sick bay aboard the ship, the crew was exhausted. Not knowing what was going on out at Atka, Lt. Amme, with our crew, a doctor, and medical supplies took off for Nazan Bay, Atka, which was several hundred miles west of Dutch

The USS *Casco* under steam.

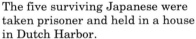

The five surviving Japanese were taken prisoner and held in a house in Dutch Harbor.

Harbor. On arriving there it was totally socked in. We could hardly find the Bay let alone attempt a landing. We proceeded to continue searching for submarines; finally the fog started breaking up, patchy, we could see into the Bay and the Casco *where she run aground to keep her from sinking.*

The sub was spotted near the entrance for the bay. Battle stations was sounded. We were fairly low—3-400 feet. The sub was very close to shore just below a small cliff. Lt. Amme banked the plane around, dove down maybe about 75 feet above the water; it happened so fast that we did not have the guns clear for the blisters. Lt. Amme dropped the combination depth charge-bombs. One hit right on deck of the sub, did not explode and bounced off. I do not believe that it had time to arm. The bomb damaged the sub; when it went into a dive and started evasive action, it was leaking oil, creating an oil slick, its progress could be followed by this slick. Smoke flares were dropped along this slick. Destroyers in the area were alerted by radio; alerted, they followed our smoke flares, took over using sonar, located the sub, and depth charged it. That was really a sight—the water looked like it was electrified form the depth charge blast. The sub surfaced, the destroyer crew captured several prisoners. I understand that these were

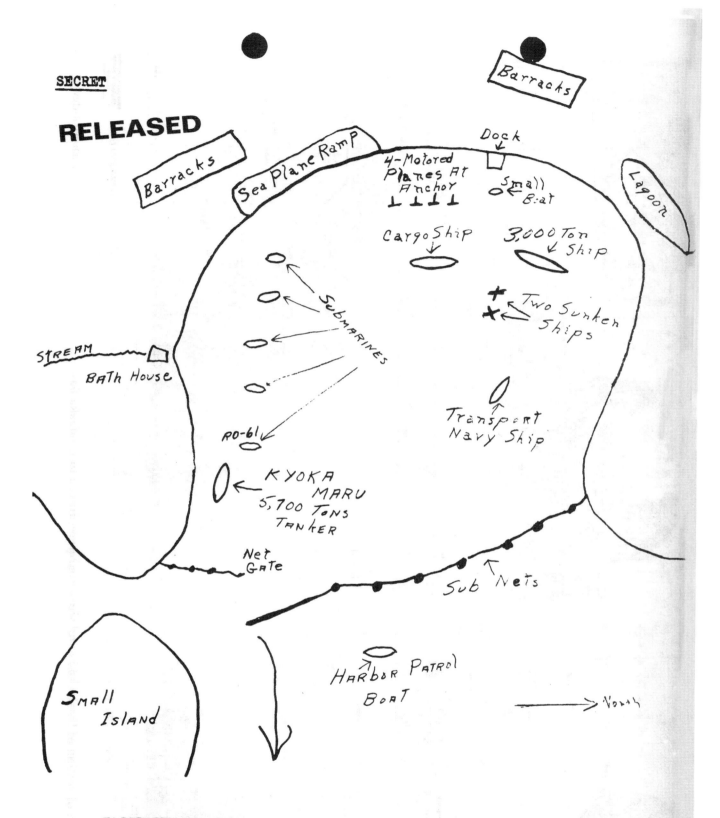

RELEASED

95

Barracks

Barracks

Sea Plane Ramp

Dock ↓

4-Motored Planes At Anchor
⊥ ⊥ ⊥ ⊥

Small ○← Boat

Lagoon

Cargo Ship ↓

3,000 Ton ↓ Ship

Submarines

Two Sunken ← Ships

STREAM

BATH House

RO-61

Transport ↑ Navy Ship

KYOKA MARU ← 5,700 Tons Tanker

Net Gate

Sub ↑ Nets

Small Island

Harbor Patrol Boat ↑

→ North

FACSIMILE OF CHART OF KISKA HARBOR WITH SHIPPING AND INSTALLATIONS AS SKETCHED BY YOSHIO USHIKADO, TORPEDOMAN - 2ND CLASS, JAPANESE NAVY. SKETCHED AT DUTCH HARBOR, ALASKA, SEPTEMBER 8, 1942.

some of the first Japanese prisoners of WWII taken alive. The picture with the crew was taken as Lt. Amme was recommended for a medal.

Carl "Bon" Amme VP-43 *

Arne Havu, (Amme's) copilot, noted that it was clearing up near Mt. Korovin for about 100 yards offshore. He looked back out of the side window and saw another PBY at a lower altitude (Coleman's), then suddenly saw the conning tower of a submarine surfacing directly ahead of the other plane.

Phil (Andy) Anderson, copilot to Coleman, saw the submarine about the same time. Havu and Anderson bounced around in their seats, yelling to their respective plane commanders. Both reacted immediately. Amme made a tight 180° degree turn and saw Coleman commence his bombing run. Two depth charges straddled the submarine.

The attack on the *Casco* had a ripple effect. It was the main tender for the western end of the theater. At least one PBY was on patrol and left without support.

Calmer V. "OLE" Olson VP-43

I was a radioman aboard PBY #4466. We were on extended patrol north and west of Atka Island. Upon our return flight heading for the USS Casco *from which we had departed earlier. I received a message which stated, "Do not return to ship, we have been torpedoed." We therefore landed at Korovin Bay about eight miles across the island from Nazan bay where the* Casco *was anchored, or by now, was sitting on the bottom.*

During the night, a heavy storm came up. The storm ripped our bilges open causing us to take on water faster than we could bail it out. Ensign Decker, our plane commander, asked the crew if we should attempt to take off, a risky venture at best, or should we beach the plane and hope someone, other than the enemy, would hear our call and pick us up. As instructed by Ens. Decker, I sent out SOS messages while we were still on the water, not knowing whether they would be heard or not, or worse, heard by the Japanese.

Once on the beach, we drew straws for assignment of duties. My duty was to locate fresh water. I did in fact, find a small waterfall not far from where we were beached. Two men were assigned to cross the island in an attempt reach the Casco. *Eight miles of tundra walking was a difficult task. We bade them farewell. We made a tent out of parachute silk and laid down to rest.*

The next day we heard a ship's whistle some distance off the coast. We all agreed that it was one of ours and not Japanese. It turned out to be the USS Hulbert, *a welcome sight indeed. The executive officer came out to get us in a small boat but was unable to cross the high waves off the beach. He then shot us a line which we attached to our rubber life raft enabling him to tow us to his boat, right through the waves, by the way.*

Aboard the Hulbert, *we were treated royally. The captain, knowing we were hungry offered us anything we wanted to eat, as long as the ship carried it. I chose bacon and fresh eggs and was so rewarded.*

The Hulbert *took us to the* Casco, *sitting on the bottom of Nazan Bay. Upon pulling away from our beached boat, our marines used it for (target) practice. But as far as I could tell, they missed it.*

Upon reaching the Casco, *we were advised that the two men crossing the island had not been seen. We immediately took off in another PBY to search for our men. We located one of them on the beach, but the other man we did not find.*

We continued to operate from the Casco *until September 6 when we returned to Dutch Harbor, but I never heard about the second man. I pray that somehow he made it to safety.*

(Taken from the PatWing–4 newsletter)

IN-SHORE PATROLLING VS-49

Since the PBYs were being used for long range patrolling something was needed to scout the areas near the bases. This job fell to the single–engine 0S2-U or "Kingfisher." The 0S2-U was equipped with either a single float or wheels. Kingfishers performed what was known as "Inshore Patrol" and escorted ships passing through the area. The unit responsible for these patrols was Scouting Squadron VS-1D13, later recommissioned as VS-49. The Squadron operated 13 to 15 planes, some on floats, a few on wheels. In addition, short "utility" flights were made by the venerable Grumman J2F-6 Duck, an amphibious biplane.

Fred Joseph VS-49

During the year that I was attached to VS-49 at Dutch Harbor it was a rather uneventful time in that area of the Aleutians. The main excitement was the "cat and mouse game" that prevailed between pilot versus weather system.

Our duty was patrol and escort. Twice each day (weather permitting) a flight was made around Unalaska Island checking the shoreline, bays and coves for any subversive activity by the enemy. In addition, a plane provided air coverage to U.S. and friendly allies ships (including Russian) moving through Unimak Pass around a 100–mile passage.

All of our flights were made in Kingfishers on floats. VS-49 kept six or eight of these planes plus a couple 0S2-Us on wheels for incidental flights. An outpost base at Otter Point on Umnak

VS-49 Kingfishers on the tarmac in
Dutch Harbor N.A.S.
PHOTO VIA O. MAUPIN

Right, the versatile Kingfisher could
operate on floats or wheels. Here a
group on wheels warms up at Dutch
Harbor. O. MAUPIN

Below, a picture–perfect landing on
water.

Right, a J2F-6 Duck gets help up the
ramp at Dutch Harbor.

Below, an OS2-U on the ramp,
Dutch Harbor. Beaching of these
floatplanes was similar to PBYs.

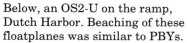

Island was manned by four or five pilots with four or five OS2-U on wheels used to patrol the shores and coves of Umnak.

Dutch Harbor provided an excellent, sheltered area for our float plane operations. Several crewmen plus a "glorified dune buggy" assisted in landing and beaching. Planes were towed forward up ramp. A short runaway alongside Ballyhoo Mountain was adequate for infrequent flights of the Kingfisher on wheels.

Our pilots, because of the weather limitations, could log a flight, either patrol or escort, on the average of one day out of three. In spite of treacherous flying conditions while I was with VS-49 we did not lose a single pilot or plane. A tragedy occurred in the summer of '44 when Lt. McElroy, an operations pilot, flew into the side of a mountain in a J2F-6 Duck, killing him and three station nurses on a sightseeing flight.

Two flights I recall being in great peril. Once on a ferry mission to Kodiak for a regular maintenance check on an OS2-U on wheels, I was flying wing on Lt. Bradley. Not far out of Dutch we flew into freezing rain, which started building a layer of ice on the wings. Any but an expert, experienced pilot such as Lt. Bradley would probably have turned back, but we pushed

J2F-6 makes the first landing on the new runway at Dutch. These small biplanes did short hops and utility flights. In 1943 a Duck carrying three nurses on a sightseeing flight, crashed killing all four aboard.

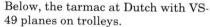

Below, the tarmac at Dutch with VS-49 planes on trolleys.

on to land at Cold Bay to refuel. There the runway was a sheet of ice, so a low and slow landing was urgent since brakes were useless. After getting out of our planes we found standing on the runway most difficult.

Once when flying a routine patrol of Unalaska Island. I flew into heavy snow. Believing it might be only a shower I maintained course, expecting to come out on the other side. After several minutes and snow only getting heavier I decided this was a major storm. Using all my "blind flying" skills and navigating to maintain a safe distance from the island, a retreat back to the east brought me back to where once again there was visual flying conditions. Eventually, I was able to pick up the welcome sight of Priest Rock at the entrance of Unalaska Bay. Priest Rock, so named because of a resemblance to a priest in a pulpit, was an unmistakable landmark for all pilots, assuring a safe haven at Dutch Harbor.

It was a funny though frustrating time on a day when I agreed to give Chief Stevens flight time in the rear seat. In order to get the OS2-U off the water, it was necessary to get the main float up on top of the water during the takeoff run—not easy to do on a calm surface. On this windless day I made three runs the length of Dutch Harbor with the 300–pound Chief and never was able to get off the water.

I experienced the perils of landing on water when returning from a flight on a day when the bay was like a mirror. Such conditions make it extremely difficult to judge distance above the water. Thinking the plane was a few feet above the surface, I cut the throttle and dropped what seemed like 20 feet. I thought the main float was coming through the fuselage! The Kingfisher was indeed a tough and durable plane.

Roy Fletcher VS-49

During float plane training at Corpus Christi, Texas. we were instructed to "sail" onto the launch/recovery ramp whenever approaching with a tail wind. This required throttling down and turning into the wind so as to "weather cock" the plane and drift downwind to the ramp. There, the beaching crew would rotate the plane nose–up the ramp and attach the beaching gear wheels to the main float. No Problem!

Now we arrive in the "Real World" at the Women's Bay seaplane ramp, NAS Kodiak. Returning from my first patrol flight in August '42, I observed the 1st Class Petty Officer Beachmaster signaling a straight–in approach. NO WAY! What's his problem, telling a brand new, red–ass Ensign how to land his ship. In spite of a fresh wind and choppy surf, by the Book I sailed in stern first to an aborted landing requiring the beach crew, up to their armpits in water, to push the plane back, rotated its nose to the ramp and attach the beaching gear, meanwhile enduring a scorching harangue by 1st Class PO Carlson and the admonition to "never no, NEVER disregard my signals again."

A group of VS-49 pilots getting briefed.
PHOTO VIA M.O.A. JACKSON COLLECTION

FURTHER ADVENTURES OF
PATROL WING FOUR

Bob Kirmse VP-41

I am really at a loss to tell you much about duty at Dutch. Flying a PBY in that area was just plain H---! Searches were usually started prior to dawn and seemed to last forever; then, the problem of returning to base, or some other mooring was awfully difficult. Even keeping warm was a problem! Sometimes we would land at the base at Umnak on metal runways, difficult because of being mud–covered and slippery, making the PBY-5A difficult to control.

Frank Browning VP-41

Airline pilots in the U.S. are limited to 80 hours of flying per month. Our pilots were flying as much as 200 hours under miserable conditions. They were very tired. One of our most experienced pilots was so exhausted he wasn't safe to fly; the Skipper had to ground him and send him home.

Hamilton Hauck, Chuck Reimen, and Jep Johnson all came to the squadron at Tongue Point, Oregon. We had gone down there from Kodiak, thinking the Jap Fleet was going to invade the West Coast. Those three had a fast course in getting their wings and were VERY poorly trained. Reimen and his crew hit a log in the Columbia River, crashed and burned, killing all. Jep ran into a mountain in the Aleutians. He was killed but some of his crew survived.

Lloyd Black VP-41

I can recall on a return flight, 50 feet over the water, hugging the Unalaska coast by radar when the Radarman stated to the PPC, Ens. John Stewart, "You're crowding it." Looking out, I could see rocks under the wings. The PPC put the PBY into a port skid. We had to reverse 180° go through Umnak Pass and come around the island and make an approach from the east and north side.

I remember many times when I was navigator, my PPC, John Stewart had to fly 50 feet off water hugging the Unalaska coast on radar, trying to get into Dutch Harbor. I disliked that approach. One time we could not make it. We turned around, flew through Umnak Pass and followed the coastline south of Unalaska, past Biorka Island. When we were off the coast at Kalekta Point a williwaw hit us, almost inverting the PBY. We were in a vertical flight position with the starboard wing about five feet above the water. I made my way to the rear blister section and clung to the eight–man life raft. I truly thought we were gonna hook a wing in the water. Fate smiled on me again and many more times to come in the treacherous Aleutians.

Bill Maris VP-43 (journal entry)

July 5, 1942. After an eight and a half–hour search mission Ens. Clark made a down wing landing, went right by the Casco *on step. Decker hit Full Throttle to go around. I saw we couldn't make it, as we would most likely run into the hillside in the clouds, so I cut the engines, and we ended up high and dry on the beach. Burnt off a bunch of rivets. The next day the pilots and metalsmiths went ashore and replaced the rivets with machine screws. They dug holes on each side, attached beaching gear and a motor launch pulled the PBY back into the beach at high tide. Never a word was said about me cutting the engines, so I guess they were glad I did. At least we were alive.*

Vern Monckton VP-41

One time they thought the Japanese Fleet was out there somewhere, and, I don't know, there was probably half a dozen planes, I don't remember exactly how many, went out to look for the Fleet. We got into the fog and we never did find the Japanese Fleet. Anyway, it started to get dark, so PPC Litsey requested permission to leave the flight. Finally, we picked up an island on radar and went in and landed on the water and taxied up on the beach. It was dark so we just parked the plane.

A PBY on step zipping past the *Casco*.

The next day—why, we found out we taxied up almost into a rock bluff and there wasn't enough room to turn the plane. We had a block and tackle in the plane, and we inflated a rubber boat and went out and tied to a rock under the water so we could pull the plane back. We would make a few feet every day. Finally, after nine days, we got to where we could turn the plane around.

A VP-61 PBY crew off loads gear as they await rescue. Their plane had run out of fuel.

The Japanese had a four-engine flying boat—I guess they were flying out of Kiska with it, I don't know. They would patrol, but they always patrolled on the other side of the island from where we were, so they never saw us. We were afraid to break radio silence, because they were patrolling there, so we didn't let anyone know where we were.

After we finally got the plane turned around and could take off, why, we went back to Dutch. We had been gone so long they were getting ready to divide up all our clothes and things, because they figured we were another casualty that wasn't coming back.

Then, because the plane was shot up, we got to take it to Kodiak and have it patched up and overhauled, so that took about a week and gave us kind of an R & R there in Kodiak. One thing that we really liked downtown, you could go downtown and there was one place in town that had fresh milk, so we would go down and get some milk, and we thought that was pretty nifty.

Bob Larson VP-41

A PBY crew in the Aleutians in the summer of 1942 could count on things being pretty exciting. The assignments were often unusual, and the capability of the PBY to land in the many bays and inlets of the Aleutians made it a versatile airplane for odd jobs. On the other hand the capability of a PBY to defend itself against attacking airplanes was very poor.

One of our submarines had run aground on the southwest coast of Amchitka Island. This island was close to Japanese-held Kiska, and it was feared they might try to salvage it, once they knew it was there. The sub crew hiked to Constantine Harbor on the east side, where they were picked up by PBYs. Our mission was to take a volunteer demolition crew to Constantine Harbor and transfer them and their explosives to the shore in rubber boats. They were to hike over to the sub, plant explosives and blow it up. Another PBY would then pick them up a couple of days later. An Army colonel was in charge of the operation.

Things didn't get off to a very good start. We were assigned a P-boat that should have been in the shops for repairs. The electric starter of the starboard engine refused to work, and the engines themselves could have used a plug change and ignition work. The engine started the old fashioned way—by having one of the mechs hand-crank it with the inertia starter while standing on the top of the wing.

The trip to Amchitka was uneventful, but since the island was so close to the Japanese, we were all apprehensive. We were within range of the float fighters (Rufes) and the four-engine "Mavis" seaplanes based at Kiska, and we didn't have the vaguest idea as to when their patrols could be expected. Bill Thies, the plane commander, approached Constantine Harbor cautiously, circling the harbor and the abandoned Aleut village at the head. There were no signs of life. We landed and tied up to one of the buoys the Navy had installed several months before, and Bill cut the engines. The life raft was inflated. Half of the explosives were put in the boat, and the demolition crew started rowing to shore. The remaining half of the explosives were moved to the waist hatch for loading on the next boat trip. I was sorting out my charts and planning the trip back at the navigators position when I heard the unmistakable sound of the multi-engine airplane, "Mavis was out on patrol!"

I have heard the expression "frozen with fear" before, and prior to that time I thought it was a quaint figure of speech. Now I am convinced that it is a very real physiological thing. What a

A Japanese 'Mavis' flying boat.

spot: some of the crew was in the lift raft, half way to shore; one cranky engine that couldnt start electrically (it would take several minutes to start it manually); our waist guns were stowed and explosives were piled up at the base of the port gun.

We were really sitting ducks, all nicely set up for a strafing attack and no immediate way to defend ourselves or escape. I looked out. I could see the Mavis on an easterly course, right off the mouth of the harbor. He was only half mile away and if we could see him, he most certainly must be able to see us. I could almost imagine what was going on with the Mavis crew. "Battle Stations! We will prepare to attack"

He stayed on his course and flew out of sight! The Navy camouflage blue paint apparently did its job of concealment. The demolition crew decided to stay and continue the assignment. While the life raft made another trip, we went through the painful process of starting the starboard engine. It took two tries as I recall. Our crewman returned with the rubber boat and came on board, dragging it in behind. Thies took off without even waiting for the usual engine warm–up. As soon as the engines were warm enough to take full throttle without coughing, he took off. We were a half hour on the way home to Dutch Harbor before the panic level got back to normal.

Ed Froehlich VP-42

One time Lt. Cdr. Tetley (VP-41) on return from a patrol in a violent storm ran out of fuel and landed his PBY in a small bay on the island of Tanaga, anchored it and he and his crew were rescued and brought into Adak.

CWO Dick Gardner wanted that plane back to Adak or salvaged for parts he needed badly. So he arranged for Lt. Cdr. Tetley, copilot Ens. Johnstone, Simpson and I to go out on the USS Teal, a sea–going mine sweeper, converted to a Sea Plane Tender, to Tanaga and rescue Tetley's PBY. Weather was fairly good when we reached Tanaga, and the PBY, which had drug its anchor, was high on the beach. The USS Teal's launch took us out, but we could not get to the beach because of shallow water. We anchored the launch and planted a buoy about 50 yards from the beach. Then we needed a line to the beach to go hand over hand with a small punt. Someone had to get that line to the PBY on the beach, that was solved instantly. When I turned around Lt. Cdr.Tetley, a man

The USS *Teal,* seagoing tug assigned to PatWing 4.

among men, was stripped to the waist and was taking off his pants and shoes handing them to the coxswain, without one word for a volunteer. It was cold and the water was like ice. The ship's launch was well equipped.

Tetley tied a small white line around his waist, over the side in waist deep water, he waded or swam in some deep places to the PBY. We tied a 21-thread line to the end of the white line, Tetley pulled it in, secured it to the PBY that was well anchored in the sand. Then six of us at a time went hand over hand in the punt to the beach, then one man had to take it back to the launch. We got Tetley dried out and in blankets till his clothing reached shore. That PBY was about half full of sand and buried nearly up to hull windows. We tried our best to re-float it but failed. The hull was pretty badly damaged anyway. Tetley and I decided our best bet was to salvage it for parts, which we did. Getting the Q.E.C. (Quick Engine Change Units) out to the ship, which had to anchor about a quarter mile out in the bay, was our biggest problem. The ship's carpenter and ship boatswain mate reinforced the bottom of the punt with planks and equipped it with outriggers with empty 55-gallon drums on each side to stabilize and prevent the punt from turning over. We got the Q.E.C. down using the PBY tripod and lowered it into the punt . A long line out to the launch pulling, we skidded the punt and engine Q.E.C. over the sand into the water, and then out to the ship where they hoisted both units up and secured them and the propellers on the ships boat deck.

We worked feverishly with the weather; it snowed eight inches one night—silver fox tracks all over the place—salvaging wing tip floats, struts, wing tail surfaces, all interior equipment, instrument etc., leaving only the hull and center section too deep in sand and water. The wings control surfaces and wing tip floats etc., were secured on the fantail where two 500-gallon gas browsers were chained down. The instruments, automatic pilot, and parts were stowed in dry storage.

Well, after being out there over ten days salvaging, the last night there a storm struck with fury, early AM, still dark. The ship was trying to pull in the port anchor, waves coming over the bow, high winds etc. Something went wrong, and with a roar the port anchor and chain left the ship. I thought it tore off the bow, nearly went aground trying and getting out the bay.

Made it finally and took two days and two nights to travel 90 nautical miles back to Adak in the roughest water I've ever seen. We'd ride quartering into two waves, then the third one would break over top of the bridge of the USS Teal. In those days a Lt. had to serve as commanding officer of a small or large ship before he could advance to Lt. Cdr. I figured this young Lt. Aviator Skipper, inexperienced, would find this trip trying, if not disastrous, but his quartermaster was an old Chief Warrant Officer, and I'm sure he contributed plenty of know how to get us back to Adak. One of the 500-gallon gas browsers on the fantail, chained to the deck, was torn loose and in a matter of minutes made trash of the wings, surfaces and floats tied down on the fan tail, nothing there was saved. The instruments in dry storage, Q.E.C. and propellers on the boat deck were all we saved.

Dick Gardner was on the dock at Adak when we landed. His first question, "Where are the plane surfaces?" After a few minutes aboard he realized what we'd been through. The ships boatswain was afraid they would have to go to a ship repair facility to repair the extensive damage done by the storm.

Vern Monckton VP-41

One time there was a Vice Admiral visiting, and we had to take him from Dutch Harbor over to Kodiak. He was so drunk when he got on the plane that we had to help him in and just dumped him in a bunk. They gave us extra special flight rations. We had steak and everything. The Admiral was out cold, so we ate everything. Then he finally woke up before we got to Kodiak and said, "Boy, you got anything to eat?" One of the guys says, "Oh, yeah, they gave us a special flight luncheon, because you were along." So we dug some old fat trimmings

"Hoot" Smith enjoys a Spam sandwich aloft.
PHOTO VIA PATWING – 4 COLLECTION

that they had taken off the steaks and put them in a pan and fried them up for the old Admiral. He said, "Boy is this what you guys get all the time?" We said, "No, they gave us special stuff for you." He was eating that old fat in the sandwich.

Robert Brown VP-42

Times we would get a little uptight, someone would come up with a little "Sneaky Pete" (190 proof alcohol). I believe it was used to clean the bombsights. We would save our juice from flight, mix it and after a couple, you had no problems.

I used to volunteer for extra short flights. One time I was at Umnak when they wanted to go to Dutch Harbor. Now, at Umnak there was no beer. Some of the guys knew I was going so put in their orders. I got my beer. Everything went fine till the time of landing. The front wheel light which indicated when it was down and locked, wouldn't indicate it.

Now our skipper didn't believe in alcohol. Here I was with a load of beer, not knowing what was going to happen. The skipper was at the runway watching. Was lucky again, could just see my AMM3/c rating go by the wayside. At the evening get together that night I was informed that there were other ways to check if it was down and locked. I felt sorta foolish, but we still had our beer.

Robert Brown VP-42

One time we spotted some ships on the radar and went to investigate. I was in the blister area that time. A few minutes later I reported two aircraft coming our way, then two more. Lt. Mann started for cloud cover, real fast. We were getting ready for action when our planes disappeared. We were puzzled, till it dawned on us. What looked like planes in the distance was the smoke from anti–aircraft guns discharge. It turned out, it was our own fleet and they didn't want us snooping around until identifying us.

Bill Grizzell VP-43

One day we had gone on a patrol out towards Kiska and were returning to our base of operations. I was flying as second pilot that day and G.W. Smith was our very capable PPC. He had just left the seat and said he was going back to check the navigation. As he left, he cautioned me to be sure to stay on top of the cloud formation, because some of those clouds had rocks in them. We were aware that some of our prewar maps were not too accurate in their altitude listings and we wanted to stay clear of any mountains. Consequently, we were flying approximately 1,000 feet above the highest mountain peak listed on the map.

I was suddenly aware that we were in grave danger. Our gunner in the rear of the plane frantically hollered over the intercom to get out of here as the radio antenna was bobbing in the snow. This radio antenna was approximately 100 feet long with a red lead weight on the end of it. This was reeled out when in flight to get better reception.

As this loud startling message came over the intercom, I was looking out of the right side cockpit window and staring at the sloping sides of a snowy volcanic peak less than 50 feet below and slightly to our side. I was also looking into the mouth of this cavernous–like cave of volcanic ash and snow. Small trails of smoke were eddying from the volcano as we flashed by.

A PBY flys over a rugged Aleutian peak.

It was Great Sitkin Island, barely hidden by the fluffy clouds. The slopping sides were streaked with volcanic ash and rocks and boulders were protruding through the snow. I immediately banked away to the left as this startling and scary scene went by. Luck was with us that day, and I have always been grateful for the Big Man's Magic Wand.

Bob Spence VP-41

With PPC Carpenter we did a lot of night patrol while Doerr was still with us. At dusk, we'd take off and fly all night. A PBY on a full tank would stay up 14 hours, so we could make a long flight. The thing is you didn't want to get up above the soup, because the old PBYs didn't have an electronic altitude meter. They were purely a pressure altimeter.

Up there that was terrible, because you'd be flying along, you might be 2-300 feet in the air, on your altimeter but actually be right down on the water or you'd could be 2-300 hundred feet under the water on your altimeter and you're flying along. With a funky pressure gauge the pressure would change just going over a front.

We had the old radar that had the hay rake antenna up there, you know, and the guy had to be a magician to interpret it properly. Our guy Dowle, he was a great, great, radio man, and he contributed a lot; he saved us a few times. Our next series of air flights had sweep radar, and we got rid of the hay rake. It would slow a PBY down seven or eight knots, and you slow a PBY down seven or eight knots, well you are way down there. When we got electric altimeters, and that was all the difference in the world.

Bill Grizzell VP-43

The date in my Navy flight log—August 26, 1942. This date long was seared into my memory. Our squadron VP-43 operating in the Alaska/Aleutian area suffered a tragic episode that day midway as we flew along the Aleutian chain between Dutch Harbor and the anchor island of Attu, way out on the tip of the chain. As we passed this rugged island on our return to base, we knew we had been on one hell of a long patrol.

Flying "above the soup."
PHOTO VIA PATWING — 4 COLLECTION

A rare formation of PBYs flying towards Kiska. Note the hayrake antenna under the wing. These created a lot of drag.
PHOTO VIA PATWING 4 COLLECTION

At the same time, Lt. Hagen and his crew with First Class Aviation Pilot D.A. Million as second pilot, were flying patrol area in the vicinity of Atka Island. Lt. Hagen's plane either had engine trouble or weather dictated that he land. The landing was soon accomplished, and the sea evidently created problems that made it difficult to taxi. The USS Williamson was soon dispatched to tow the plane to a safer haven. Towing a seaplane from the stern of a destroyer is quite a seaman challenge in rough seas, and those attempting this task soon realized that it was a losing battle.

A decision was made to abandon the plane and transfer the crew to the USS Williamson, an old four–piper destroyer. The up and down erratic movement of the plane and the destroyer by the heavy seas created a precarious feat in affecting a safe transfer. Million was in the act of attempting this transfer when the stern of the destroyer came down crushing the bow of the PBY. The collision activated the arming devices in the bow causing both 500–lb. depth charges to be released. One depth charge detonated. PBY #BU 004427 was blown out of the water and the stern of the destroyer was lifted out of the water, cracking and damaging it from stern to amidships. Lt. Hagen and other crewmembers were rescued with exception of Million, Palco, and Cabral. We were told a more diligent and effective rescue could have been effected had it not been reported that Japanese submarines were in the waters and the possibility of a sub attack was possible.

As I turned in that night on the Sea Plane Tender USS Casco, Million's bunk looked terribly empty to me, since we had shared the same compartment area for berthing aboard the ship. I felt a great sense of loss and sadness at the loss of three good sailors as did our great skipper, LCDR C.B. Jones, and the entire squadron. I was flying as second pilot to Plane Commander Lt. G.W. Smith that day and heard about this tragedy while flying.

It seems that there is always some humorous even that usually arise from such tragic wartime stories. One squadron member by the name of Hosteller was in the after head of the USS Williamson at the time of the explosion. The shock of the explosion lifted him straight up, minus his dungarees, spread–eagle style, with his arms draped over the side of the toilet stall. Need I elaborate?

Willard Olney PatWing 4 Photographer

One morning I went out at about 7AM to the plane I was flying with that day, but fog was thick on the water and our pilot decided to wait awhile. We played cards, ate a second breakfast and talked for an hour or two, during which time we heard another plane rev up and take off. Sound dies quickly in fog, so when it disappeared we thought nothing about it. About 9 or 10, the fog lifted to about 200 feet, and we made ready to leave. The practice then our loop, quite low to stay in clear air, another man and I spotted something floating on the water. He reported it and the pilot went around again with everyone looking. This time there was no doubt—it was the wing–tip float of a PBY, with the wing disappearing down into the water. The pilot dropped a smoke bomb to mark the spot and then sat down, and we all returned to the Casco *to watch as a couple of small boats went out to investigate. I remember seeing pieces of broken plane being picked half out of water by cranes and by then the deck talk was that it was the same plane we had heard taking off earlier.*

While all this was going on, somebody yelled and we looked toward the destroyer and saw a Japanese plane appear out of the fog and make a bombing run—stern to bow. The ship, however, was not hit because it zig–zagged wildly and from our position we saw water spouts on the near side, then on the far side of the destroyer. Then the plane went back up out of sight in the fog, and we heard the sound come our way, as though the pilot had only then noticed the Casco. *His bomb landed on the shore, so he must have simply guessed at our location. And that was it.*

The small boats dropped their pieces of wreckage, returned and we set off with the destroyer for a wild night of "evasive action" in a very heavy, stormy Bering Sea. My bunk was aft and the top one, with a steel beam a few inches above my head. All that night I watched it seem to move of itself close to my face, then recede, hour after hour, in time with the rattle and boom of the screws coming half out of the water in those monstrous swells. I think I finally slept.

Next day, we found ourselves back in Nazan Bay and continued with our flights—halfway down to Hawaii sometimes and over to the 180th. I never once saw a damned thing in that endless empty ocean!

In addition to patrolling duties, the PBY was designed to act as a search and rescue craft. In what became known as "Dumbo" missions, PBYs were able to locate downed planes or ships and land on the water nearby to pull the survivors aboard. Due to the extreme cold of the North Pacific Ocean, survival was measured in minutes unless crews could get into life rafts. Locating drifting rafts was extremely difficult but most flyers had faith that a patrolling PBY would somehow see them. On June 19, Rob Donely was piloting his PBY north of the chain. The day before, a B-24 had ditched in the Bering Sea 100 miles short of Umnak's airfield. They had been on a bombing mission over Kiska and had run out of gas.

The fantail of the USS Williamson. Two rows of depth charges sit in racks on the stern. PHOTO VIA W. OLNEY

Robert Donley VP-42

Because of the attrition of plane crews during the Japanese attack on Dutch, we had been ordered to do our patrolling in search of the enemy ships during the night hours. We would take off during the waning daylight hours, fly the search sector at night and return in the early morning, landing in the daylight. I was on one of the night patrols on June 19-20, 1942.

On my return leg one of the crew members sitting in the aft blister spotted a Very light. A Very light is shot from a Very pistol high into the air and gives a star like signal of distress. I told the crewmember to keep his eye on the spot and I turned the plane to investigate. Several more star shots were fired, enabling us to get closer to the source. Dawn was just breaking when we located a life raft with a number of occupants. As we circled, we tried to contact our base without any luck. We continued to circle until the daylight was enough to see the water. The sea was running with swells about five to six feet, and the wind was in a reasonable direction in regard to the swells, so I decided to take a chance and land. Fortunately, we made the landing OK and within a short distance of the life raft.

As I recall there were six men in the raft (members of a B-24 crew that had gone down on the 19th) who we took aboard. The next chore was to take off. Having spent all night using up our load of gas, the plane was relatively light, which was to our advantage. Getting up to take off speed in the swells of an ocean is like riding a bucking bronco, and once you get there you kiss off the top of the swells until you are airborne. It was a rough ride. I estimated our position was about 60 miles south of Scotch Cape (Unimak Island). From there we proceeded on to our base at Cold Bay, landing on the Marston Matting runway. We were flying a PBY-5A (amphibious). Some of the crew administered first aid, though I guess none of the men were seriously injured. I was told two of the crew of the B-24 went down with the plane. I didn't get to talk much to the B-24 crew, except to find out their plane commander was a fellow named Wintermute. When we landed at Cold Bay they got off the plane in a hurry and as I recall didn't even say "thank you." However, we knew they appreciated the ride. Anyway, by that time myself and my crew were very tired, and all we wanted to do was to report in and go to our tent for a little shut–eye. We did that with a great deal of satisfaction of a job well done.

Frank Browning VP-41

We lost Jules Raven and his crew. John Herron had landed at sea when he got lost in the soup and was low on fuel. "Ham" Hauck had located him and stayed with him all night while waiting for the tender, flying circles overhead. When Hauck got low on fuel, Raven relieved him on station. When the tender arrived with fuel, Raven headed for home. It was getting dark, and I expected him to land at Umnak, which was clear. But he was scheduled for the mail run to Kodiak the next morning, so he tried to reach Dutch Harbor. By the time he learned Dutch Harbor was closed with heavy ground fog, he didn't have the fuel to return to Umnak. We transmitted a signal for him to home in on, as he requested. Then his radio was silent. An Army Lookout Post reported seeing a big flash to the north. A search at daybreak found no trace. It was another tragedy.

A PBY lands to rescue a B-25 crew. They have released a dye marker and smoke signal to mark their position.

A SALUTE TO VPB-136

In late August, 1942 the U.S. moved west by building a base on Adak Island. Within three weeks a functional, albeit rudimentary, airfield was in operation. By draining a shallow lagoon the engineers were able to create a flat area large enough to use for the air field.

This brought the Army and Navy planes 400 miles closer than Ft. Glenn on Umnak Island. The planes of the Eleventh Air Force and PatWing 4 spent the winter concentrating on bombing the Japanese off of Kiska and patrolling Aleutian waters for enemy ships and subs. Periodically, the Navy would send a small fleet to bombard Kiska. These forays were usually hampered by weather and had little effect on the Japanese.

In addition to Adak, another base was built on Amchitka in February 1943, only 60 miles away from Kiska. Amchitka was one of the few flat islands of the chain. It also lacked a decent harbor. With typical ingenuity, the engineers built an airstrip and began attacks against Kiska from there.

Off loading supplies on the beach at Adak. A new base was established here in September 1942.

The airfield was built on top of a lagoon. This led to flooding problems.
PHOTOS VIA PHPC COLLECTION

In spring 1943, VP-41 and VP-42 were sent southward. Behind it left VP-61 and 62. The war had progressed and the squadron was getting some rest and was replacing the PBY's with the first issue of PV-1 Vega Venturas. They were re–designated as VP-135 (VP-42) and VP-136 (41). The PV was faster, sleeker and more maneuverable. They also operated only on wheels. No more ditching at sea when the bases were fogged in or a plane was hit by enemy fire.

Robert R. Larson (Former Patrol Plane Commander with VPB-136)

In a way, VB-136 was a reincarnation of VP-41. The slow, vulnerable PBYs were traded in for hot, new PV-1 Venturas at Whidbey Island NAS early in 1943. Commander Nathan Starr Haynes was the last skipper of PBY Squadron VP-41 and the first skipper of Ventura Squadron VB-136. Easy going Brad Brooks was the Exec. The first order of business was to check out and train in the Vega Ventura.

The first airplanes were originally scheduled to go to the British, and they were configured for a single pilot. Kits were obtained to convert them to a Navy two–pilot cockpit, and the

Left, a PBY lands in the muck, Adak NAS.

Below, a PBY lands on the new strip at Amchitka, 60 miles from Kiska.

The replacement for the venerable PBY, the Lockheed PV-1 Ventura.

copilots seat was obviously an afterthought. He was uncomfortably cramped to the right sidewall, and he had no flight instruments to read. If the copilot were required to fly on instruments, he would have to gaze over to the pilot's side. He did have a wheel and rudder pedals of his own but no brake pedals. Since the Ventura had no flight engineer's station as on the PBY, all the engine controls were installed near the pilot. He now had to read fuel gages, temperatures, pressures, and handle the engine mixture and anti–icing controls in addition to the usual prop pitch and throttle controls. He also had a two–speed supercharger, a new factor which became useful in all–out escapes from Zeroes later on. The power turret with twin fifties which didn't run out of ammunition right away—our PBYs had 15 seconds worth—was also a welcome feature.

Most intimidating to the old PBY pilot was a tremendously complicated fuel system. Instead of the two tanks of the PBY, he was faced with 11 tanks, a maze of valves and fuel transfer possibilities that defied understanding. Further, there was a shortage of handbooks which gave you a clue as to how the system worked.

I was lucky enough to get my ex–PPC (Patrol Plane Commander), Bill Thies, as an instructor in transitioning into PVs. Bill had barely checked out in them himself, but he had explored the flight characteristics quite thoroughly. During the first demo flight, he said, "Let me show you how nicely this recovers from a spin!" whereupon he pulled the wheel way back and kicked full right rudder. I hadn't been in a spin since primary training at Corpus Christi. I had never been in a spin in a multi–engine airplane. I got pretty puckered as the airplane responded with a sharp roll–off to the right and the nose pitched sharply down. We did about a half turn spin then Bill recovered it smartly. Aileron control was effective at all times, due to the wing slots ahead of them. I must say it was a good confidence-building maneuver. The PV had two 2000–HP Pratt and Whitney engines, as compared to the 1200–HP engines of the PBY. At light training weights, we felt that the airplane had power like a fighter, and the acceleration and rate of climb were pretty impressive to ex–PBY pilots.

Our crew consisted of two pilots, a radar-radio operator, a turret gunner, and a crew chief who doubled as a "tunnel" gunner. The pilots were expected to do their own navigating, but *this proved to be awkward. The navigation table was located in the cabin right on top of the cabin fuel tank. To get to it, one of the pilots had to get up and walk back to the table, do some navigating, then return to his seat. We solved the problem by teaching some volunteer enlisted men to do some DR–type of navigating and man the table. Since I was the navigation officer of our squadron, I set up a classroom, established a curriculum, and did the instruction. The navigator trainees were very eager to learn this new skill, and they worked out very well.*

After three months of training, VB-136 was ordered to the Aleutians. VB-135 (formerly VP-42) had preceded us by about three weeks. We flew up to Annette Island in several groups, each holding a rather loose formation. After gassing up at Annette Island, we proceeded to Kodiak, and there we got our first initiation to the capricious Alaskan weather. Storm clouds built up in front of us, and we got lower and lower to stay in contact conditions. I was in a group with Commander Haines in the lead, and he disappeared into a rain squall ahead of me. I immediately made a 180–degree turn and started climbing to get on top of the clouds. A radio conversation with Hutchinbrook radio range told me that the Valdez airfield was still clear and would be that way until I got there. After setting a new course for Valdez, I noticed that I had acquired a new wingman. It was our skipper, Nate Haines. Since the Valdez airstrip was rather short—about 4,200 feet—it was a tight fit for the PV. "Pink" Morrison was the only one who made it into Kodiak that day, and that was done by staying close to the water and barging ahead. Visibility was terrible, but he managed to see Kodiak airfield before he hit any of the nearby mountains.

We started patrolling out of Adak. VB-135 had been sent on to operate from Amchitka. Being old PBY pilots, we tried to operate the PV in a similar fashion, low to the water. That proved to be hazardous. We lost Permenter and Malloy who crashed into the water. We nearly lost Bill King, who made a very low approach and hit the water, but he managed to pull up in time. His airplane sustained some severe damage to the tail. From then on we tended to fly above cloud layer and diligently practiced our instrument letdown techniques. The PV could change altitude very fast and flying it close to the water like a PBY was definitely hazardous.

After some months of rather uneventful patrols, our fearless wing commander, Commodore Gehres, decided to go after the enemy. Half of the crews of VB-136 were selected to transition into Army Air Corps B-24s, with the ultimate objective of conducting raids on Paramushiru, once the bomber airfield on Attu had been built. The remaining crews would continue to carry out the patrol work. For those of us on patrol duty, this meant flying nearly every day with no rest in between. I logged a lot of PV time during that period. Several crews did check out in B-24s and managed to get some time in them. However, when senior Air Corps generals got wind of the scheme, they declared that if any bombing missions were performed, they would be done by Army Air Corps crews, not by the Navy. Gehres' plan was cancelled, and VB-136 once more was up to strength for patrol missions.

In a sense, one casualty did result from the B-24 training program. "Throck" Throckmorton,

 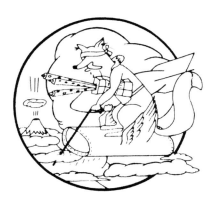

the one who drew the funny cartoons of Aleutian life, was one of the B-24 trainees. Throck drew up the first VB-136 insignia, which was "Bugs Bunny" riding a bomb. He had not flown a PV for a couple of months, so he took one out to re-familiarize himself. His PV was seen to take off, then plunge into the water shortly after becoming airborne.

His elevator trim tab was found to be in the full nose down position. At that time, the trim tab sense was not "natural"—the direction you turned the knob was not oriented to the airplane response. We conjectured that he had forgotten which direction to turn the trim tab handle and had inadvertently cranked it to the full nose down position when he had meant to put in nose-up trim. His time in the B-24 program had caused him to lose familiarity with the PV control system, which cost him his life.

Operating at Adak had one disadvantage. We were constantly under the watchful eye of Commodore Gehres. If he didn't think we were getting airborne fast enough, he would send the duty officer to find out what was wrong and chew us out. We tended to get even by flying low over his hut after takeoff, in full high RPM and high power, making as much noise as possible.

Our skipper, Nate Haines, was intrigued with the idea of bombing Kiska through the overcast, using our ASD radar, which gave a kind of distorted picture of the land features underneath. He planned to approach Kiska Harbor from the North, in order to get the best radar picture.

The big day arrived, and five VB-136 planes approached Kiska in formation. The only trouble was, it was clear and unlimited visibility, and we did not have the expected cloud protection. Anti-aircraft shells began to explode among us, very close! We dropped our bombs and immediately made a hard, diving turn but not before going right through one of the black, ugly puffs. Fortunately, no one was damaged seriously. VB-135 at Amchitka got further involved with radar bombing and would lead fighter-bombers over Kiska.

In August of 1943, a combined Army–Navy landing operation was set in motion to retake Kiska. Six VB-136 PVs were formed as a torpedo strike group and sent to Amchitka to stand by. The PV bomb bay could not accommodate a torpedo internally, so we had to fly with the bomb bay doors open and with the torpedo hanging half out. After the torpedo was dropped, the doors could then be closed and the airplane cleaned up for a high-speed retreat. My log book shows that we flew from Adak to Amchitka, then ten days later returned to Adak.

This page, 500–lb. GP bombs are loaded on a PV-1.
Opposite page top, a trio of PVs make landfall somewhere in the Aleutians.
Opposite page bottom, the landings on Kiska, August 1943.

Bill Thies VP-136

I was assigned temporary duty with Colonel Frederick's Special Service Force for the invasion of Kiska. I was in charge of a communications group to call in air support. At H minus something or other, while sitting on a troop transport off the west side of Kiska, we got reports that a firefight was in progress (during the night). Turned out that each point of the pincers movement had met each other not knowing each were friendly forces, and we lost about 20 men from "friendly" fire, but in the meantime we thought there was a battle going on with the Japanese.

The USS *Abner Reid* was damaged
by a Japanese mine off Kiska. The
entire stern was blown off.

Left, the official caption says these
PVs were supporting the landing at
Kiska.
Below, nose wheel failure on the
runway, Dutch Harbor.

At dawn, I climbed down a rope ladder to get into a landing craft. As I was doing that, the ass end of a destroyer about 400 yards away blew up in the air. (Scared the hell out of me!) We thought a Japanese 5–inch shore battery had hit it. Turned out that the tin–can had backed down on a mine. I hit the beach armed with hand grenades, carbine, .45, and a very dry–mouth. My orders were to proceed east until we met the enemy. Well, we plowed eastward until I was in the Japanese campground on the east side of Kiska and radioed the Fleet Commander that there were no Japanese there. The fleet came around on the east side and we "occupied" Kiska.

Bob Larson VP-136

Thick fog at Amchitka prevented any flying during the period that we were backing up the Kiska landings. The Japanese had abandoned Kiska a week or so before the landings, and our help was not needed to repel any enemy fleet. When the bomber field at Attu was finished in October 1943, VB-136 was sent there, becoming the first PV squadron to operate out of there. Shortly after we arrived, the Japanese sent a welcoming committee of six "Bettys" who made a bombing run on the airfield. Our defenses sent up an impressive array of anti–aircraft fire but no hits. I heard that a P-38 managed to shoot one down, but most of them got away. The Japanese sent patrolling Bettys from Paramushira, and it was inevitable that sooner or later we would meet one when we were on patrol. John Conners saw one and gave chase, but the Betty is pretty fast, and Conners stopped the pursuit when his fuel got low. "Sandy" Dinsmore also spotted one on his patrol. He closed to extreme range and fired his bow guns until they got too hot. Some damage to the Betty was noted, but it managed to escape.

We had one pilot, "Hap" Mantius who was a bit of a maverick. Commodore Gehres was of the opinion that bombing missions to Paramushiru with the PV-1 were not practical, an attitude that we did nothing to change at the time. Hap was determined to prove that it was within the range of the PV. By using manual mixture leaning and flying at long range cruise speed, he got within sight of Paramushiru and took pictures. Hap became the first one to fly to the Kuriles and back. He had no bomb–bay tank at the time. Future PV flights would be made with an aft bomb bay tank of gas and the forward bomb bay equipped with three bombs. Not enough fuel remained to make it to any but nearby alternate airfields, so a good weather forecast for Attu was a firm requirement of those who did the missions.

VPB-139 finally showed up and relieved VB-136 in December 1943. Were turned to good old USA for leave, rest and recreation. VB-136 deployed for the second time in June of 1944. This time we had new PV-1s with another cabin fuel tank, a true copilot's position with a more comfortable seat and flight instruments. Three more .50 caliber machine guns were added in a "chin gun" installation. We also got a third pilot who acted as the navigator.

Three .50 cal. "chin" guns added
needed firepower to the PVs.

PVs in their revetments on Attu.

120

LCDR Charles Wayne was the skipper, with Lt. Ed Hayes as Exec. Larson, Nelson, and Morrison, the pilots with the most Aleutian experience, were PPCs from the first deployment. Several senior officers were assigned from flight training bases to round out the roster.

VB-136 left for Attu in June, 1944, under ideal weather conditions. Most of the squadron arrived at Attu in good shape. However, one PV-1 made an emergency landing on the Japanese strip at Kiska, only 3,200 feet long. For a PV-1 that is tight! The plane had to be almost completely unloaded and defueled to get it out of there.

With the extra fuel tank, missions to Paramushiru were a little more practical, so VB-136 was assigned to do both daylight bombing and patrol missions. LCDR Wayne was most eager to establish a reputation as a gung–ho bombing squadron, so we did missions on a pretty regular basis. On one of the first missions, Lt. Lindell found that after some time maneuvering near the target, he did not have enough fuel to get to Attu, so he became the first VB-136 pilot to land at Petropavlovsk. Second to go to "Petro" was John Dingle, who was shot up by Japanese fighters. Third was John Cowles, who was severely damaged by ground fire and fighters and had to make a crash landing on a Russian beach. Finally, Wayne himself had an engine shot out over the target and had to land at Petro.

Because Russia was not at war with Japan, it could not be seen giving aid to Japan's enemy. Therefore, Americans who crashed on Russia would not be simply returned. Instead they were "interned" and after many months were shipped back out of the U.S.S.R. via Iran and eventually back to the Aleutians. Most were proud of their trip around the world.

After the loss of four crews, VB-136 was relieved of further bombing missions and reverted to patrolling. Lt. Price had a close call on one mission and very nearly didn't make it back. During his attack on Paramushiru his airplane was hit by ground fire, and a pushrod housing on one engine was hit. His engine started losing oil but at a slow enough rate so that he thought he could make it back to Attu. Oil pressure was monitored very closely. About half way back, the pressure got so low that the propeller started to act up and would not hold a steady RPM. He decided to shut down the engine, feather the prop, and proceed on the remaining good engine. A rescue PBY was sent out to meet him in case he had to ditch, but Lt. Price made it back to Attu OK.

Lt. Littleton made fame by becoming the first PV-1 to shoot down an enemy fighter with his bow guns. A Japanese "Tony" was making a head–on attack on him, so he raised his nose and gave the enemy fighter a burst from his five fifties. He got a picture of the Tony trailing smoke. One other special mission was notable. Aerial photos were needed of proposed invasion sites on the west coast of Paramushiru, so three VB-136 crews, Lt. Morrison, Lt. Nelson and Lt. Bacak were assigned the job. This was especially hazardous, because this put enemy fighter fields between them and their escape route. To avoid detection, they flew low over the Kamchatkan peninsula (which the Russians objected to through diplomatic channels), then made a three–plane formation high speed run, taking pictures all the way. The mission was very successful, and they had achieved a complete surprise. No enemy fighters got even close.

VPB-136 (formerly VP-136) was finally relieved by VBP-139 in March 1945 and proceeded to the USA. One more airplane was lost on the way home. Lt. Moorehead, with some passengers as well as his crew, got lost on the way to Kodiak. It was easy to do with all the false courses and swinging beams that were characteristic of the old low–frequency radio ranges of that time. They were particularly unreliable at sunset when Moorehead was supposed to arrive. He ended up ditching the airplane off the fishing village of Karluk on the southwest coast of Kodiak Island. All were rescued by a boat from the village, but all of their baggage was lost. One bright note. It was generally considered that Moorehead had the worst–looking Aviation Greens uniform in the Navy. He lost it in the ditching and was forced to buy a newer, much more presentable set. That was the last notable event of VPB-136. The war ended, and VPB-136 was eventually decommissioned.

Bill Thies VP-41

I think Frank Browning was a passenger on a flight I made from Kodiak to Whidbey Island, Washington in a broken down PV-1. The only thing that worked were the engines.

We got into a hell of a storm off Tatoosh in zero/zero visibility. I wasn't sure I was at the entrance to the Straights of Juan de Fuca, but gambled and headed East. Lost my nerve and started circling 50 feet above the water and prayed. After about ten minutes and getting low on fuel, the clouds opened VERY briefly, and a ray of sun came through, and I saw the lighthouse at Neah Bay. I knew where I was. Then it socked in again, but we continued east and broke out at Whidbey. When we landed the tower called and said I was losing gasoline and it was pouring out onto the runway and to evacuate right now!

When we got out, I didn't smell gasoline, so I scooped some of the liquid up and it was salt water! We had been flying so close to the water that the vacuum in the bomb bay sucked up full of water! The Lord has been very good to me ! That's the last I ever saw of the Aleutian Islands.

The men of VP-41 on sandbag duty, building shelters on Mt. Ballyhoo.
PHOTO VIA PATWING 4 COLLECTION

BIBLIOGRAPHY

122   Amme, Carl H. and Pat Wing Four Reunion Committee. *Aleutian Airdales, Stories of Navy Flyers in the North Pacific During WWII.* Plains, MT: Plainsman Publishing, 1987.

Cloe, John. *The Aleutian Warriors, A History of the 11th Air Force & Fleet Air Wing 4.* Missoula, MT: Pictorial Histories Publishing Co., Inc., 1991.

Cohen, Stan. *The Forgotten War, A Pictorial History of World War II in Alaska and Northwestern Canada,* four volumes. Missoula, MT: Pictorial Histories Publishing Co., Inc. 1981.

Freeman, Elmer. *Those Navy Guys and Their PBYs: the Aleutian Solution.* Spokane, WA: Kedging Publishing, 1984.

Garfield, Brian. *The Thousand Mile War, World War II in Alaska and the Aleutians.* New York: Ballantine Books, 1969 (since reprinted by the University of Alaska Press).

Morgan, Lael. *The Aleutians.* Edmonds, WA: Alaska Northwest Publishing Co., 1980.

Rearden, Jim. *Koga's Zero, the Fighter That Changed World War II.* Missoula, MT: Pictorial Histories Publishing Co., Inc., 1995.

Scrivner, Charles L. *The Empire Express.* Temple City, CA: Historical Aviation Album, 1976.

Unalaska High School Students. *The Aleutian Invasion, World War Two in the Aleutian Islands.* Unalaska, AK: Unalaska City School District, 1981.

This terrazzo floor design was put in the Bachelor Officers' Quarters at the Naval Station. It is now on display at the Museum of the Aleutians.

Above, Nine "Kate" bombers were part of the second attack on Dutch Harbor.
FILE PHOTO

Below, a grouping of PBYs on the runway, NAS Dutch Harbor, September 16, 1942.
NATIONAL ARCHIVES, 80-G-215262

An OS2U scout plane coming up to
the ramp at Dutch Harbor,
November 11, 1942.
NATIONAL ARCHIVES, 80-G-386611

Snowstorm at Dutch Harbor, August
15, 1942.
NATIONAL ARCHIVES, 208-AA-5UU-1

J2F Ducks at Dutch Harbor. The
place was a standard utility aircraft
in Navy service since 1937. It was
stationed aboard battleships and
cruisers as a command plane and
also used as a photo recon plane.
ALASKA STATE LIBRARY
HERVEY THORNTON COLL. PDA 338-528

THE AUTHOR

Jeff Dickrell arrived in Unalaska, Alaska, in 1990, from Naperville, Illinois, to teach high school history. Immersing himself in Aleutian history, especially the WWII era, he is a board member of the Museum of the Aleutians and a researcher for the National Park WWII Interpretive Center in Unalaska. An annual class trip to Washington DC has allowed him much access to the National Archives Still Picture Division. In 1997 and 1999 the Patrol Wing Four Association invited Jeff to their reunion where he had a chance to meet with the many veterans he had been corresponding with for this book. He continues to enjoy the friendships made there. Jeff has a B.A. in History from Northern Illinois University. When not in front of a class or his computer, he can usually be found paddling his kayak or hiking the hills of Unalaska.

125

THE COVER ARTIST

John Hume's interest in aviation started at a very young age, and he has been researching, sketching, and painting airplanes for over 25 years. As a 34–year resident of Alaska, his main subject tends to be historical Alaskan aviation, but other areas of interest include the Korean War, the Cold War, and airliners from the 1940s, 50s and 60s. His work has been published in a variety of aviation magazines and books. Many of his paintings can be found in the Alaska Aviation Heritage Museum, the Air Force Art Collection, and private collections around the United States. His most recent work is a collection of paintings featuring American fighter aces from the Korean War.

THE MUSEUM OF THE ALEUTIANS

Museum of the Aleutians

PO Box 648
314 Salmon Way
Unalaska AK 99685
Phone (907) 581-5150
FAX (907) 581-6682
aleutians@arctic.net
www.aleutians.org

The Museum of the Aleutians opened in 1999 in a new building which was constructed on a World War II foundation. The museum presents the culture and history of the Aleutian and Pribilof Islands from prehistory through the Russian–American period and World War II, to the present. In the Permanent and Changing Exhibit Galleries are a wide range of archaeological, ethnographic and historic artifacts reflecting the unbroken human occupation of these islands for more than 9,000 years. The museum is a private, nonprofit corporation supported in part by the City of Unalaska, the Ounalashka Corporation and the Aleut Corporation and through membership fees, grants and private donations.

ALEUTIAN VETERAN'S INFORMATION

126

Name _____ Military Serial Number _____

Dates of service in the Aleutians _____

Rank during Aleutian Campaign: _____

_____

Unit(s) served with in the Aleutians:

_____

Description of duties while in the Aleutians _____

_____

Bases or Islands stationed on _____

_____

Method of transportation for arrival and departure _____

_____

Type of quarters   Impressions of Quarters _____

_____Barracks   _____

_____Quonset Hut   _____

_____Yakutat Hut   _____

_____Tent   _____

Impressions of Food _____

_____

Impressions of the weather _____

_____

Recreational Activities _____

_____

Please share a copy of this information with the Museum of the Aleutians.